The Social Epidemic of child abuse

★★★

Some Other Titles From New Falcon Publications

Aha! The Sevenfold Mystery of the Ineffable Love —Aleister Crowley
An Insider's Guide to Robert Anton Wilson —Eric Wagner
Bio-Etheric Healing —Trudy Lanitis
Undoing Yourself With Energized Meditation and Other Devices
Secrets of Western Tantra: The Sexuality of the Middle Path
Dogma Daze —Christopher S. Hyatt, Ph.D.
Rebels & Devils; The Psychology of Liberation—Edited by Christopher S. Hyatt, Ph.D.
Aleister Crowley's Illustrated Goetia, Sex Magic, Tantra & Tarot:
The Way of the Secret Lover, Taboo: Sex, Religion & Magick
Christopher S. Hyatt, Ph.D., and DuQuette
Pacts With The Devil, Urban Voodoo: A Beginner's Guide to Afro-Caribbean Magic
—Jason Black and Christopher S. Hyatt, Ph.D.
The Psychopath's Bible —Christopher S. Hyatt, Ph.D., and Jack Willis
Ask Baba Lon —Lon Milo DuQuette
Aleister Crowley and the Treasure House of Images
—J.F.C. Fuller, Aleister Crowley, Lon Milo DuQuette and Nancy Wasserman
Enochian Sex Magic and How To Workbook
—Aleister Crowley, Lon Milo DuQuette and Christopher S. Hyatt, Ph.D.
Enochian World of Aleister Crowley —DuQuette and Aleister Crowley
Info-Psychology, Neuropolitique, The Game of Life, What Does WoMan Want?
—Timothy Leary, Ph.D.
Nonlocal Nature: The Eight Circuits of Consciousness —James A. Heffernan
on What is —Ja Wallin
Rebellion, Revolution and Religiousness —Osho
Reichian Therapy: A Practical Guide for Home Use —Dr. Jack Willis
Shaping Formless Fire, Seizing Power, Taking Power,
The Magick in the Music and Other Essays —Stephen Mace
The Illuminati Conspiracy: The Sapiens System —Donald Holmes, M.D.
The Secret Inner Order Rituals of the Golden Dawn —Pat Zalewski
The Why, Who, and What of Existence Vlad Korbel
Steamo Goes to Havana, The Social Epidemic of Child Abuse
Michael Miller, M.Ed., M.S., Ph.D.
Woman's Orgasm: A Guide to Sexual Satisfaction
—Benjamin Graber, M.D., and Georgia Kline-Graber, R.N.

Other Titles by J. Marvin Spiegelman, Ph.D.

A Modern Jew in Search of Soul
Buddhism and Jungian Psychology
Catholicism and Jungian Psychology
Hinduism and Jungian Psychology
Mysticism, Psychology and Oedipus - A Small Gem
Protestanism and Jungian Psychology
Psychotherapy and Religion at the Millennium and Beyond
Psychotherapy as a Mutual Process
Reich, Jung, Regardie & Me - The Unhealed Healer
Rider, Haggard, Henry Miller & I - The Unpublished Writer
Sufism, Islam and Jungian Psychology
The Knight - A Small Gem
The Nymphomaniac
The Quest - Further Adventures in the Unconscious
The Tree of Life - Paths in Jungian Individuation
The Wisdom of J. Marvin Speigelman Vol. I - Selected Writings
The Wisdom of J. Marvin Speigelman Vol. II - Psychology and Religion

Other Titles by Dr. Israel Regardie

A Garden of Pomegranates
A Practical Guide to Geomantic Divination - A Small Gem
Attract and Use Healing Energy - A Small Gem
Be Yourself - A Guide to Relaxation and Health
Ceremonial Magic
*Dr. Israel Regardie's Definitive Work on Aleister Crowley,
    The Eye In The Triangle*
Healing Energy, Prayer and Relaxation
How To Make and Use Talismans - A Small Gem
Israel Regardie's The Foundations of Practical Magick
My Rosicrucian Adventure
Mysticism, Psychology and Oedipus - A Small Gem
Practical Magick - A Small Gem
Teachers of Fulfillment
The Art and Meaning of Magic - A Small Gem
The Body-Mind Connection, A Path to Well-Being - A Small Gem
The Complete Golden Dawn System of Magic
The Complete Golden Dawn System of Magic Book 1 - Ltd. Edition
The Complete Golden Dawn System of Magic Book 2 - Ltd. Edition
The Complete Golden Dawn System of Magic - The Black Edition
The Eye in the Triangle: An Interpretation of Aleister Crowley
The Golden Dawn Audio CDs, Vol. 1, Vol. 2, and Vol. 3
The Legend of Aleister Crowley
The Magic of Israel Regardie
The Middle Pillar
The Philosopher's Stone
The Portable Complete Golden Dawn System of Magic
The Tree of Life
*The Wisdom of Israel Regardie - Vol. I
    Selected Introductions, Prefaces and Forewords*
*The Wisdom of Israel Regardie - Vol. II
    Selected Essays and Commentaries*
*The Wisdom of Israel Regardie - Vol. III
    Selected Articles, Introductions, Prefaces and Forewords*
What You Should Know About the Golden Dawn
Wilhelm Reich, His Theory And Techniques
Aha! (Dr. Israel Regardie and Aleister Crowley)
Roll Away The Stone/The Herb Dangerous
    (Dr. Israel Regardie and Aleister Crowley)

MANY OF OUR TITLES AVAILABLE ON KINDLE!
Please visit our website at http://www.newfalcon.com

Copyright © 2023 Michael Miller

All rights reserved. No part of this book, in part or in whole, may be reproduced, transmitted, or utilized, in any form or by any means, electronic or mechanical, including photocopying, recording, or by any information storage and retrieval system, without permission in writing from the publisher, except for brief quotations in critical articles, books and reviews.

ISBN 13: 978-1-56184-507-1
ISBN 10: 1-56184-507-8

New Falcon Publications First Edition 2023

The paper used in this publication meets the minimum requirements of the American National Standard for Permanence of Paper for Printed Library Materials Z39.48-1984

Printed in USA

NEW FALCON PUBLICATIONS
2046 Hillhurst Avenue
Los Angeles, CA 90027
www.newfalcon.com
email: info@newfalcon.com

The Social Epidemic of child abuse

★★★

EXPLORING THE ROOTS OF VIOLENCE
WITHIN THE AMERICAN FAMILY STRUCTURE

by

Michael Miller, M.Ed., M.S., Ph.D.

NEW FALCON PUBLICATIONS
LOS ANGELES, CALIFORNIA, U.S.A.

Table of Contents

Chapter 1 The Cursing of Our Children — 1

Chapter 2 The American Family and Psychological Violence: A Synchronous Social Phenomenon — 9

Chapter 3 The Roots of Abuse — 17

Chapter 4 Abuse vs. Neglect — 49

Chapter 5 Causal Theories — 69

Chapter 6 The Family as the Cause of Abuse — 79

Chapter 7 Some Case Examples of the Intergeneration Transmission of Abusive Behavior — 89

Chapter 8 Treatment and Prevention — 105

Chapter 9 Identifying and Understanding Child Abuse — 117

Chapter 10 Epilogue — 127

Chapter 1
The Cursing of Our Children

Verbal Abuse: Our Exposed, Secret Shame
The Effects of a Declining Culture on the Mental Health of Our Children

No child has ever signed a contract to be born.

How children are treated and regarded is the best metaphor that **reflects** the true moral development of a culture.

When asked what type of adults we want our children to become, we say one thing.

When we observe how our children are raised, we see a different paradigm being applied.

When we observe how our children turn out, we revert back to our original model of expectation.

We frequently explain away this glaring disparity by denying our failure and blaming the young adult, thus reinforcing the entire socialization process–itself schizophrenic in nature–and which a puritanical and at the same time hedonistic America is so famous for throughout the world.

We single out America because it claims to be loving and forgiving; it claims to be the best; setting the world standard of excellence in every facet of human life. From economics to *socialization; from production methods to technology. (Forget "Science", the discovery of new knowledge and the creations that spring from it; the products of an enlightened people. We never had "Science" and never will. We have "technology": the bigger faster, cheaper, more of the same basis of excess consumption.) Americans also **believe** we should export goods; are also **determined** we should export our "values." And when our "values" are rejected by other cultures, we then extol the "might makes right" excuse to use force to insure our concept of "human rights" for all, while our own society spirals ever further down into the abyss of a cesspool.*

*But the fact is, as our daily newspaper headings show, America trains its citizens to be **violent, deceptive and abusive**. Not simply to ourselves and to adult peers, but to children. In reality "The American Dream" promises, violence, deception, and abuse is **the** way! Everyone "knows"…**how else can you be successful?***

No Child Can Say "No" To Abuse

When I was a young child and someone called me a name, I would say, "Sticks and Stones will break my bones, but names will never hurt me." But the fact is, names did hurt me. But the pain was hidden. It had to be hidden, and I was the one who **had** to do the hiding. After all, I was taught it was a sign of weakness to let others know their purposely designed cruel words "Hurt!" And if for some reason, I "lost my senses" and opened myself up to them and let them know of my pain, I risked the further pain of humiliation by the "cowardly act" of letting them know that I was hurt and wounded by what someone said. It was not until the mid 1960s that a daring realization began to enter the minds of a few perceptive, analytically-minded individuals: that **words have as much power to produce an effect on a human being as does a physical force on a material object**. After all, words are very real forces arising within the brain. They can be displayed on the cathode ray screen of an oscilloscope, and charted to a strip-chart recorder's paper. In short, they are a form of **energy**. And as such, they have the power to elicit emotions: the physically-based, chemical **effect** of the thought that **caused** it. In turn, these emotions produce actions by effecting the neuro-physical basis of our nervous systems, which then drive the rest of our material bodies to act on physical reality. Knowing this, all controlling societies apply this knowledge to create fear in their citizens. They do this through the use of fantasy and imagination, not so thinly veiled in their propaganda based, guilt structured, dependency-oriented legal system, itself generated by the socially determined edicts of the "chosen few," whose names and faces neither we will never know or see. In so doing, they guarantee obedience by the cheapest of all possible methods; since words are free.

From a more workable daily point of view, words or "names" are the basis or soil from which many human interactions spring. Sociology, psycholinguistics, hypnosis, neurolinguistics, semantics, and propaganda have realized the overwhelming power of language in determining human behavior. In fact, Psychologists use words as their primary method of understanding, analyzing, and treating the mental causes that lie behind behavioral disturbances…or the physical "acting out" of these "thought-energy" generated effects.

If You Do Not Believe in the Popularity of Psychological Abuse, Then Turn On Your Television

And yet with all this theoretical and applied knowledge, little is said about the effects of words on the outcome of our child rearing practices; except of course, to refrain from swearing, demonstrating the most flagrant sexual actions, and editing the most violent and brutal movies.

The reason for this? Because all of us are guilty...in one way or the other...of abusing others with our own words.

While words may be cheap and always at the ready, they are nonetheless more powerful than we care to realize or admit...**especially** to ourselves.

"Words are everything and everything is words."
–Sheriff Leroy Baca
Four time elected Sheriff of Los Angeles County

Words As a Component of Psychological Abuse

Unlike the ever-prevailing stereotype that portrays minorities and the poor as the exclusive social elements behind physical and mental child abuse, it is our position that Psychological Abuse has no social status whatsoever and neither does it have any cultural boundaries. Rather, it is our contention that such abuse is actually the most common form of derision indulged in by the middle and upper classes. The tragedy of this of course, is that unlike physical scars that heal, the insidious effects of psychological abuse remain buried in the psyche, often festering for decades, disturbing all elements of the individual's life throughout his or her entire lifespan.

It is the power of psychological abuse to so invade the entire field of a child's life and mutate, thus producing a plethora of negative thought patterns, that simply pointing a finger at specific "incidents" as "common examples" has become a nearly impossible. Surprisingly, in most cases, victims of such abuse are not even aware that they have been abused. This miasmatic characteristic of the abuse–while certainly not the most graphic and horrifying form of injury–is yet the most permanent and devastating of all forms of pain; simply because it is both non-incidental and nebulous at the same time. And being amazingly common, it does not lend itself to either simple investigation or healing. In fact, psychological abuse is as normal in America as cannibalism is in some primitive, tropical societies. The operational focus behind this analogy then, is that *the abusive-arrogant American does not regard his or her behavior as deviant, anymore than does the cannibal.*

Psychological Abuse is So Common in America That It Has Become a Way of Life

Psychological abuse has become a way of life in America. Its practice–and its consequences–are everywhere. As a long time coach, I have never been a guest in someone's home– where I did not observe psychological child abuse in one form or another. I well remember observing a mother calling her 3-month old child a "bad boy," simply because he was throwing up his milk. The woman was white, intelligent, and had a college degree, and financial means.

Having experienced life for so many decades, in anything but a "social vacuum," I have seen children beaten, humiliated, called derogatory names, belittled in front of other children and with adults present–simply because the parents were embarrassed by the child's behavior in what they considered to be a "public" setting. What does it communicate to us, about ourselves–as individual beings–and as a so-called "cultured, advanced civilization," when professionals and journalists agree that the "reprimand" (abuse) of a child is "required," and simply argue as to whether it is best to spank the child or simply scold it? What does it tell us about "loving" parents who demand respect because they do not have the courage to deal with their own shame, or handle their adult-centered problems in a mature, rational way? *These* are the "adults" the child is to look up to and later, emulate? Is our stature as human beings so insignificant, that emotional pigmies are giants compared to us?

Psychological abuse—whether in the home, on the job, or in the street—is so rampant and accepted as "normal," that we do not recognize it as an illness; as a disease that is destroying the very values and ideals which we mouth as being so important to our "civilized" way of life.

Animal Welfare Is More Important Than Child Welfare In Mainstream America

In this "America," there appears to be more public concern about animal welfare than the effects of psychological abuse. The slightest physical or even verbal reinforcement needed to train an animal so it can live among human beings without causing harm to them or their property, has seen legislation of one form or another enacted: all from "Animal Rights Activists" determined to "stop the abuse!" Yet these same "activists" think nothing of deriding, insulting, and down casting their own offspring in order to "train" them to live "properly" among the same set of human beings they are–in effect–protecting their animals from!

At times, clinicians, bureaucrats, and other so-called "socially responsible" and "politically correct" individuals and groups, refer to the progress made in child welfare by referring to Public Law 93–237 which defines abuse and neglect as:

> the physical or mental injury, sexual abuse, negligent treatment, or maltreatment of a child under the age of eighteen, by a person who is responsible for the child's welfare under circumstances which indicate that the child's health or welfare is harmed or threatened thereby.

It is true that this law acknowledges the issue; but in our opinion, this acknowledgment is both microscopically narrow and caustically vague. "Narrow," in that this law primarily implies parental or family abuse; "vague," in that the guidelines that detail the **content: that which actually constitutes** "abuse," is left as a matter of individual interpretation. In addition, these laws and many others dealing with this issue are woefully lacking, in that they do not adequately cover the abuse sanctioned by agencies, or society at large. Further... and most appalling of all—is that they do not emphasize *psychological violence* as the most common form of abuse. And finally, it is our contention here, that this and other so-called "Public Laws" do not provide for adequate remedies so drastically needed to turn the tide of this incredible social epidemic.

Chapter 2
The American Family and Psychological Violence: Synchronous Social Phenomenon

Another indication of commonness of Psychological Abuse in America, is the sparseness of research in this arena. As a consequence, in order to accurately convey the violent nature of the American family and culture that stems from it, we are forced to use data which only *reflects* the level of physical violence within the family structure.

It is important to remember, that the lack of an effective definition of abuse–as well as the societal lack of awareness of psychological abuse–interferes with any exact reporting. An additional complication is caused by society's reluctance to interfere with the "sanctity" of the American Family–a syndrome commonly referred to as "The Closed Door Effect." Nevertheless, the official statistics published by Statista Research Department, January 27, 2022, found that approximately 618,399 children nationwide *were reported* as abused or neglected.

While physical abuse and violence are obviously of paramount importance, it is our position–taken from our patient population–that probably no-more than 10% of children actually experience intense and or chronic physical violence.

Judging from our experience, we also estimate that while close to 30% of children experience corporeal punishment in some form–which includes the proverbial "laying on of the hands"–**almost all** children in America experience one or more forms of psychological violence.

It is quite clear then, and we cannot begin to overemphasize, that Psychological Violence is the result of belief systems; thought patterns that have their origin in the history of a given culture. These ideas, attitudes and beliefs frequently function unconsciously. That is, out of the stream of conscious awareness; and as such, they are "automatically" accepted as being natural and necessary, thus making them difficult to erase.

The paucity of research into psychological violence masks the fact that most of us are psychologically violent. Even researchers and clinicians do not wish to be exposed to their own shame and guilt, which results when they recognize the face beneath their own masks.

Self-guilt is one of the reasons research in the area of psychological violence has been so neglected. This, of course, stems from the fact that at one time or another all of us have all been guilty of harming the esteem and self worth of someone we love. And this is particularly true in the area of child rearing.

I recall speaking with two doctors who couldn't understand why their own children were having more problems then is normally expected from teenagers. When I asked them if they considered the issue of psychological violence as perhaps being at the root of their children's problems, they responded by saying that they never spanked their children, and then jokingly stated that perhaps that was the problem! I next asked them how their expectations for their child's success was communicated. Both responded that they told their children, over and over again, how important it was to be successful. Following this, I asked each of them how much quality time and emotional support they gave to their kids. Their reply? "Their careers took up most of the time during their kids early childhood." Yes, and they also expressed the regret that they could not spend more time with their children, even now, while the teenagers' problems were escalating.

Finally, I asked them if they ever punished their children. Both doctors responded with complete acknowledgment. I then asked if they called them names, humiliated them in front of friends or family, made comparisons to other relatives., etc. Again, both responded, "Yes."

I explained to them that most people have done the same with their own children, and that it was now my opinion that in so doing, the children are harmed psychologically. I continued my delivery by saying that–once again, in *my* opinion–this was only the tip of the iceberg; and in fact, the entire socialization process in America is violent and abusive, and that we–as professionals in this very human field–are so immersed in it ourselves, that we can not even see it when it is pointed out to us.

A Working Definition of Psychological Violence

No doubt, the reader has noted our switching back and forth between Psychological abuse and Psychological violence. This reason for this is not scientific; but rather, to impress upon the reader's mind the inescapable conclusion that *Psychological abuse is violence*.

Psychological Abuse (or, Psychological Violence) consists of, but is not limited to:

- Name-calling (personal derision)
- Prophesying (predictions of the child's failure and his or her inevitable non-acceptance by peers, family, friends, and society in general, owing to this "failure")
- Differential treatment of siblings (through both verbal and physical acts demonstrating favoritism of one child over the other)
- Exposing children to scenes of verbal or physical conflict ("fighting") between the parents
- Emotional unavailability ("I'm too busy now! I have to have this report done by the morning," or, "I've been on my feet all day! I need my own time")
- Teaching metaphysical ideas and concepts which a child cannot understand ("I don't care if you don't like church and you don't know what it means. It's good for you. You'll understand what it's all about when you grow up!")
- Yelling (loud verbal deliveries, purposeful fear-inducing tactics mean to elicit obedience)
- Destroying toys and punishing pets (frequently seen by small children as extensions of themselves)
- Comparing (establishing scales of "good and bad," "acceptable versus unacceptable" between two children or children's normal actions of growth)
- Isolation ("You don't deserve to be around me. You're not good enough," or, "I have something more important to do, or someone more important to see than you")
- Requiring the child to fulfill parental needs (my love for you is conditional upon what you do for me)

- Threats of the withdrawal of love ("My love for you can be removed at any time. You have no security unless I decide to give it to you, and then, if I decide to give you my love, it will be on my terms! But watch out! I can withdraw it at any time. **You** are dependent upon **Me**, and upon doing as I say at **all** times!")
- Bizarre punishments (being locked in a closet, or having food withheld)
- Threats of abandonment and institutionalization
- Withholding correct information ("**You** need **My** view at all times. Your own view is worthless without **My** input, because I have *special knowledge*.")
- Substituting family fictions for facts ("Our family reality is not what you see and interpret for yourself, but what I say it is: you are incapable of thinking and understanding for yourself")
- Setting a course for the child's life without considering its own needs, wants and talents
- Making the child wait in terror for the consequences of an action (delayed punishment, meant to increase the level fear, often for the parent's own amusement, either conscious or unconscious)
- Belittling ("You are not worth the room you take up, or the effort and money I give to raise you.")

While the contents of this book are painful and depressing, we believe that by society's being made aware of these painful facts, accepting them and their conclusions, we can indeed step out of the darkness of our violent ways, and into a brighter and healthier future.

In the spirit in which our country was founded, we must once again embrace the causes of our discomfort: regardless of how uncomfortable that embrace might prove to be. It is up to us–that **each** of us that becomes aware of these tragic conditions–to reach down as well as out, in order to find the courage needed to consciously change the situation that is destroying our society more and more with each passing day. A courage that will not only rejuvenate our culture, but help Mankind to become that which we intrinsically know we are capable of becoming.

The assumptions which govern this book then are:

1. That it is fundamentally wrong to physically, sexually, psychologically (emotionally, mentally, and interpersonally) abuse children.

2. That children are not the property of the State, their parents, or any other authority. They are, in fact, autonomous living beings that require the finest care we can conceive of during their earliest and formative years.

3. That as parents and adults, we can authentically function only in the roles of nurturers, guardians, teachers and friends, providing children with the tools necessary to develop their own true potentials, and to live their own lives according to their own best judgments.

4. The prevention and treatment of child abuse is of paramount interest and importance. Intercession into the outmoded, and dangerous beliefs, values, and ideas that lead to the horrors of all forms of child abuse, is the goal of every thinking adult, regardless of his or her social position and status.

5. The treatment of children in general, and that of older children, i.e., those of the late teen years, who come from dysfunctional families, is a matter of fundamental importance, and is an issue that all mental health professionals must address.

It is of vital importance for the mature reader to understand that the psychopathological difficulties we have outlined above, as well as the references made to what we deem to be "normal behavior," are both simply the results of the beliefs that we, as a people, hold to. In other words, as we see it, what we refer to as "mental illness" and "mental health," are in actuality the result of beliefs that are held by a given section or culture of humanity. And in our case, the belief system model used in America, is based almost exclusively upon Psychological Violence. Both polarities–the model of mental illness and the model of mental health–are nothing more than the opposites of each other, the referent frame for **both** being the underlying belief system of the nation. Further, from the studies we have seen, and which we have quoted here, it is clear that this violence is a neither random nor diffused; but rather, constitutes the statistical norm in this society in our country.

Thus the base of almost all "mental illness" and addictions, is Psychological Violence. Further, it is but a small step in realizing that the immediate origin of this violence is the American Family unit itself, which has its historical roots in both the Puritan ethic and in long time hedonistically-based philosophies.

Chapter 3
The Roots of Abuse

In the 2021 Prevent Child Abuse America survey on Physical Punishment, 87% of adults reported experiencing physical punishment at some point in their childhood. Nearly one third of all respondents reported physical punishment at least a few times a month as a child. Yet 45% felt it is sometimes necessary to discipline a child with a good hard spanking.

(From *Physical Punishment: Attitudes, Behaviors, and Norms Associated with Its Use Across the U.S.*, Prevent Child Abuse America, 2021. J. Bart Klika, Julia M. Fleckman, and Melissa T. Merrick)

Child abuse is not a new phenomena. Both in Biblical times and in early America, what we now openly refer to as child abuse, was viewed as being completely normal. Indeed, it was not only popular, but was actually accepted as a reasonable form of adult behavior. Beside the more common forms of such abuse, there were also less obvious forms of this violence model. One instance, for example, was seen daily in the treatment of young female children. Their role relative to adult society, and to other children even of their own peer group, was that of chattel. A part they obediently played out for centuries, and which only recently has been exposed before the general public as a valid, deeply scaring form of family abuse and violence.

Research has been done which confirms the abysmal fact that Clinicians in private practice tend not to report cases of psychological abuse when it arises from patients who share a similar value system with the clinician, or who are of the clinician's race or class. It is only when the government realizes that the majority of the adult population—which includes the middle class and wealthy—are as guilty of child abuse as are those groups termed, "minorities." Only then can public pressure be brought to bear upon the federal structure to devise programs that can help put an end to this epidemic.

The roots of abuse are buried even deeper than may at first be supposed, in that they lie in the very concept and history of the Family unit itself. The Family structure, which has been portrayed for generations as centering around the wife and child management, is itself laden with many clichés, descriptions, and prescriptions, which–upon closer examination–are found to sanction infanticide, the exercise of physical brutality on women, and a constellation of child abuse measures supposedly designed to "insure the proper rearing of an obedient child and good citizen."

And not surprisingly, the "blueprint" for this model of violence is found within the Bible itself. It takes only a cursory reading of any part of the Old Testament, for example, to find such numerous Biblical references to this type of violence, that we have chosen to reference some of the examples in their own section. But beyond this perhaps "expected" source of recommendations for cruelty in general and child abuse in particular, lies a code of "child- abuse guidelines" that few Americans are aware of. We are speaking here of the old "Blue Laws;" those edicts that specifically sanctioned brutality and violence against children.

For example, the Blue Laws of Connecticut specifically stated that a father could kill a disobedient son (Blue Laws of Connecticut, 1861, Section 14, p. 69). Massachusetts statue (1646) reflect the fundamental chattel attitude; a child over the age of sixteen could be put to death if he was "stubborn and rebellious and will not obey his (parents') voice and chastisement..."

While most of us would not sanction such a law in so-called "modern times," the fundamental attitudes behind such laws still exist, and are indeed practiced by the majority of parents in this country. That is, parents today have the "rights of discipline" which not only include corporeal punishment, but more importantly, include the "right" to say and teach anything they wish to a child.

The reader is no doubt aware that latter laws such as these had their origin in both the Old and New Testaments, whose teachings emphasize the master- ownership relationship originally established by the early priests and prophets. The relationship of this authority- oriented hierarchy–which they envisioned as existing between their vision of God and man–was then expanded and applied by them to the more familiar structure of human society, That is, it was directed to the generalized Male/female relationship, as St. Augustine so beautifully emphasized when he stated, "Women ought to serve their husbands as unto God." Of course, as time progressed and human society became more complex, this Biblical model was extended to include Male/child relationships, until finally, in modern times, it was extended to include the Parent/Child relationships.

It is also worth noting that in its essence, the Chattel model referred to earlier, has become the dominant model upon which the government-citizen relationship as it exists today, is based; and that it is practiced by virtually every civilized western government. In short, it has become the defining lens through which governments view their citizens, and the matrix through which they interact with those citizens. And amazingly, this master-servant paradigm has been willingly accepted by both parties, as television coverage of an national election will clearly illustrate.

Parents become parents by having children; but having a child rarely makes a parent either an adult, or an expert on child rearing.

One way to curb child-abuse is to recognize that parenthood conveys *no rights* whatsoever. On the contrary, it produces nothing but *obligations*, of the most difficult kind.

Parents have children because they have a biological drive to procreate. The consequence of this naturally occurring drive is that the act of having children is not for the benefit of the child. On the contrary: it is for the benefit of the gene-pool, the parents' need to feel "biologically fulfilled," and to serve the purpose of the state.

If we wish to mature as humans and within our civilization, our orientation must be shifted to a child-centered, not adult centered context.

Obviously, children are not responsible for the acts of their parents; and this particularly includes their birth. Yet many children are blamed for the problems their families face, while constantly made to feel that these problems are due to their– the child's–very existence. What is so tragic, is that the child has no way to defend his or her emotional structure against such outright such lies and irresponsible adult statements and suggestive actions.

These same children, one-hundred percent innocent as children, become one-hundred percent responsible for the pain and misery they live with as adults, and which they then impose upon their own children. "The sins of the father..." are thus visited upon the next generation of children. This twisted form of "logic"–viewed as "logic" because it is never questioned or examined by society as a whole, but rather, patently accepted–makes no sense whatsoever. It is thus both a convenience and a contrivance, albeit a necessary one if the status quo is to be upheld. In the dysfunctional, toxic culture, that calls itself "America", anything becomes possible–and has.

The position of this book is that all dysfunctional families and relationships are a result of one of the many forms of a chattel model. For instance, in America, the husband is often regarded as the Lord (Owner) of his family, thus reinforcing the tendency in nature for the smaller, the less powerful, the weaker, to be the victims of abuse. Put simply, in daily practice, members of the American family are not regarded as being equally human. Such psychological brutalizing of children and women is a phenomenon that even such "macho" male figures, such as Tom Cruz and Sylvester Stallone would not tolerate. At least, not on the screen.

The ownership of property allows the owner certain rights–and requires certain well-defined responsibilities–all, prescribed by law. This includes the use of the property, the care of–or lack of care of–the property, the freedom to change the structure and image of the property according to existing social and moral, and "common sense" codes, and the right to dispose of the property. While all of us superficially believe that none of these property rights are applicable to human beings, our attitudes and demonstrated actions contradict this in most of our own relationships. From the beginning of time, the ownership of human beings was a common right given to nobles and victors in battles. As we progressed from barbaric practices to more civilized ones, we gradually gave up the direct or outright ownership of human beings. In fact, America was one of the first countries which overtly banned the ownership of humans. That is of course, unless they were of different races. When black slaves were finally "freed" of direct ownership, the country settled down to more sophisticated, universally accepted, never-to-be-questioned forms of ownership, such as the continued ownership of wives and children by their husbands. This ebb and flow, pendulum-like process continued unabated throughout the late Nineteenth Century, until the advent of the indirect ownership of workers by the corporation. Unions were the next social phenomenon to make their effect felt on the fragile corporate-worker interaction, adding further restraint, constraint, and responsibilities to the manufacturing interaction, complicating the issue of "property ownership" still further. This does not even take into account the civil rights movement that helped blacks and other minorities to gain more freedom from the "human ownership" model upheld throughout the end of the Civil War. As society continued to examine and re-examine itself over the last century, women finally began to benefit to some degree, as illustrated by their right to practice birth control, have abortions, and work competitively along side their former "owners." Yet no matter how much oscillating progress has been made in these issues, the opening years of the 21st century continue to illustrate the predominant attitude toward both women and children: they remain the property of both their husbands and the government at large. It is our belief and contention that as long as these members of society are still tacitly and overtly regarded as property, and are "owned" in either a psychological or emotional context, the entire human race remains in a condition of enslavement.

It is our position then, that children and spouses must be treated with the same respect and dignity that we would automatically extend to valued guest in our home. Because if the truth be known, in this sense we are all "simply guests." You would not attack the personality of a guest you invited for dinner. Nor would you slap her, lock her in a closet, or ignore her. In this sense also, an infant must be viewed as an "invited guest," if her parents and society at large wish to regard themselves as civilized people, having genuine self-esteem, instead of the Madison Avenue blotted variety. How can we accomplish this? By replacing the word–image commercial characterization of women and children with common sense, caring, realistic behavior that emboldens all parties concerned, and which allows for the equal growth- potential of all people. The era of brutality–of psychological and physical abuse–in which we regard people as chattel and personal property–is over. And we as individuals and members of a larger social structure, must hold ourselves accountable for insuring that it remains this way.

If treating children with respect and dignity is too difficult a requirement for potential parents to seriously entertain, it would be far better for the prospective parents, the would-be children, and for society, if those children were not produced. For the sword of having and rearing children cuts both ways, unknown to most parents and prospective parents. What do I mean by this statement? Simply this. That in all of my years of interacting with parents while coaching, I have noticed that many parents lose more self esteem through their poor and abusive child-rearing habits, than they do by violating almost all other personal and cultural values.

What is new today however, is the media attention given to abuse, as well as professional and governmental interest in the phenomenon. Unfortunately, this attention has a rather broad range. From the misinformed "news-every-half-hour" and witch hunt media coverage, to the well researched studies and institutional-directing, mandatory abusive behavior, reporting.

The Witch hunts scenario is perhaps the most curious of all. No doubt, because it has so much "public appeal," a problem in itself, in that it feeds back on, and supports, the abuse issue directly.

These "media hunts" focus on "fringe" religious groups, drug users, and self-proclaimed Satanists as the offending parties. The purpose of such media attention is two-fold. First, to de-focus the viewer away from the actual problem–what we as a country believe, how we live, the values we uphold, those we conveniently discard, and how this value-set and its consequential actions actually form the foundational aspects of abuse. Second, by categorizing the fringe religious fanatics, drug abusers, etc., as the diseased element responsible for children and female abuse, the conscience of a nation is thus appeased, as the "average, good citizen" is encouraged to "keep vigilant" for the evil ones who create the nightmare world of abuse. It is but a small, unconscious leap for the "average, good citizen" then, to equate a mother trying to move her screaming, tantrum-throwing child along, with a secret satanic worshiper, who "must be reported"–or worse.

The government as well, has an active role in perpetuating child abuse. Although it has a vested interest in protecting children from direct exploitation and violence, all too often it refuses to directly interfere with the direct upbringing of children. In point of social fact, governmental rules–which legislate and mandate virtually every area of the individual's life–are so archaic in this area of human concern, that it has no requirements established for any individual to become a parent. While yet insisting and persisting publicly that "...today's children are tomorrow's future." As this statement is obviously true, our future as a nation and supposedly "free people" looks very bleak.

If the purpose of government is to serve its citizens by providing for the equality, safety, and rights of all, then mandatory education and testing must become the essential criteria for parenthood qualification. Our view in this matter is firm; simply owing to the fact that human beings–when faced with any new task–must first of all unlearn deleterious thought-patterns and the subsequent negative behaviors that arise from those patterns as a matter of Cause-and Effect. These same individuals must then be trained in the basics of thinking and acting, just as anyone would in order to assume the responsibilities of a difficult, demanding, and exacting task. Such "schooling" could only produce qualified parent applicants who–upon bringing new life into the world–would then justifiably regard themselves *and* their offspring with the greatest pride and esteem.

As we have pointed out, while government is continually preoccupied with regulating everything from jay-walking to day and health care, it has not–and as of the time of this writing–addressed the issue of child abuse in any significant manner. As the reader is all too aware, it simply refuses to move beyond the confines of allowing anyone and everyone to breed as indiscriminately and as callously as they choose. The rearing, welfare, education, and specialized moral and ethical training of the children thus produced is left to either the "parents," or to the state agencies it has created, due to its complete failure to address this crisis-issue. It is clear to us, that if our government continues to legislate and control all other aspects of our lives, it will surely reach the point where there will be nothing left to regulate. Perhaps then, it can get on with the work that needs doing, and which underlies the decline of this nation: that of dealing with psychological abuse and human *responsibility*, as opposed to its current concern of "rights" for the most outlandish behaviors and people that is plaguing our society today. If it does, perhaps then it may eventually come to understand that it is not simply Russia and the China which must more fully and effectively embrace and act upon the principles of democracy, kindness, gentleness and genuine human rights, and do so in a more effective manner. It may even come to recognize its own charade in mouthing conveniences, as opposed to implementing corrections that will truly provide for "Life, liberty, and the pursuit of happiness" for all of its citizenry.

As it stands now, in essence, the philosophically-based, functional aspects of our government that are in use on a daily basis in those matters it deems to be of vital concern, are equally applied to the child abuse issue in a very real global sense. Specifically, people are regarded as essentially stupid, dangerous, "necessities" who require constant control. As the ruling authority, government also assumes that the nature of those to be controlled is rooted in either evilness, fundamental stupidity, emotional instability, or intellectual inferiority. Of course, the only response from such a government-held attitude, is an abusive, paternalistically centered reaction. It is rarely understood by the government practicing such a philosophy, that its own paternalistic foundation are based upon its own evil intent, ignorant views, emotionally instability, and intellectual incapacity. Ironically yet understandably, the only time such a governing system is capable of seeing these negative aspects of the paternalistic attitude, is when it "righteously" points an accusing finger at other historical paternalistic models.

In an early attempt to escape the obvious conclusion that socialization and religious training were fundamentally violent and hateful in and of themselves, early researchers and therapists assumed that family violence and abuse were aberrations only, reflecting the individual pathology of a few individuals. And more recently, television propagandists, spurred on by government, have been selling the view that drugs and alcohol are the "root causes" of abuse. This disturbing "catch- all" idea follows from the fact that alcohol and drug abuse are often associated with violent behavior particularly in the lower classes. However, as further investigation illustrates, and as statistical associations demonstrate, these negative social conditions are not the exclusive–or even fundamental–causes underlying the abuse issue.

It my opinion based upon over 40 years of life, psychological, and coaching experience–that alcohol and drug abuse, like child abuse, are nothing more than the by-products of a toxic culture. They are *"fundamental effects,"* not *"fundamental causes."* For example anthropologists have demonstrated that the behavior of intoxicated individuals is a function of situational variables and is, in fact, primarily a consequence of learning. What many of today's social scientists are aware of but are reluctant to admit, is that our socialization process is the fundamental cause of our personal, social, and national ills: all of which are–in one way or another–abuse issues directly, or which can be traced to an abuse issue with very little effort.

As to drug and alcohol abuse issues themselves: our newfound national interest in this subject has shed little light about the abuses' ultimate top-layer concerns: what it is costing us as a nation, and how to effectively control it. Yet our "war on drugs"–which at best strikes at one scant part of the underlying cause–still retains massive political, public, and individual attention, all of which is brought to bear upon only those most obvious of external elements that perpetuate the problem. Meanwhile, our as yet undeclared war on child abuse means that we continue to ignore the root causes which produce substantive, destructive, human results. Yet the government has the audacity to produce television infomercials and ads in which they pretend to instruct parents on raising their children?

The answer is as simple as this. What government, parents, and social agencies alike must be made to realize, is that abused children become abused adults. And abused adults become abusing parents, criminals, drug addicts and dysfunctional people in all walks of life.

As we strove to prove, abuse is the primary cause behind most of our economic woes, national levels of mental illness, psychosomatic disorders, and our overall general failure as a proximal human culture. Indeed, as a people we have shown that it is much easier for us to give money in a vain but convenient attempt to "cure" a problem, than it is for us to give the love, respect and compassion needed to effect a genuine and complete cure. Indeed, little or nothing is being done about the root cause of this tragedy; and the reason for this is obvious: we as a society are still in the denial stage. Because this thesis is so important, we will repeat it: The reason for the perpetuation of this tragedy is clear: as a society, we remain in the stage of denial.

Child Abuse Is Rampant.
No Child Can Simply Say "No" to Abuse.

Eighty-seven percent of Americans sampled believe that strong discipline is necessary for raising children. But the sad, unrecognized fact is that...

Obedience Is Not Discipline

This single word, "discipline," has been misused and abused beyond recognition of its original meaning, and the proper context in which it can be productively employed. The word is actually derived from the word, "Discipline," meaning a follower or exponent of someone: as in, Biden was at one time a disciple of Obama.

In contemporary society however, this word is now used to justify every form of heinous crime against children. It is a word–substitute for the parent admitting that she/he is either ignorant, or frustrated; stressed, or stupid; or fearful–usually of their own incompetence in dealing with life–issues. Or it is simply employed as a convenience in the parental exercise of bullying the most helpless members of their own or others families. For when such people use the word "discipline," a feeling of safety is automatically generated within them; one that allows them to perpetrate their criminal child-abuse actions, unabated. They feel safe, because society itself–and its religious foundations–are the models that provide the very sanctioned methods for the child rearing practices in which they engage. In short, in America, the word "discipline" is on the same cultural footing as the flag, baseball or "mom-and-apple pie," since all "good" Americans believe in these "tried and true ideals." But unlike the mom-and-apple pie metaphor, no two people, groups of people, institutions, or organizations, use the word to mean the same thing. And the reason for this is that the "average American" simply does not understand what "discipline" is all about. This condition is publicly demonstrated nearly every day; primarily, by the very news media that have taken it upon themselves not only to look after our general welfare, but to "educate" us in what is "right." Such an example can be found in the evening television program in which child discipline is discussed. The host and the "expert" begin the discussion by agreeing that discipline in child–rearing is necessary. And the show concludes with the host and "expert" agreeing that discipline is necessary. Yet at no time throughout the presentation, did either participant define the concept, its purposes, its uses, or its limitation.

If you were to go as far as to ask an adult what "discipline" meant, and further ask him or her to give you an example of a parent applying this concept to a child in the child-rearing process, what type of concept-application model do you think would emerge from their response?

In a small study that we conducted along this line, we found that the responses did not fit the standard definition of the word, "discipline," which is "Training which corrects, molds, or perfects." Rather, the responses given by the parents properly belonged to the concept of "obedience" that is, "The willingness to obey, regardless of the content or purpose of the demand." When this was pointed out to the participants, they were neither surprised nor troubled. When they were then asked "what" their child was being taught to be obedient toward, their first response was to provide explanations containing such phrases, "for the good of…" or "without discipline how will he or she fit into society?" Unknown to the parents, the last statement of "fitting into" is correct; but not in the way they meant. The problem is much more global than their simple replies would have them or us so easily believe. For in order to make children "fit into" a violent, crime-filled, self-destructing society, the children most definitely must be taught–not *obedience* itself–but the ***appearance of obedience***. This is the only way they can survive: by ***mimicking*** adherence to the rules, regulations, and laws of a social, cultural, and governmental system that has failed. It is important for the reader to remember, that in this case, the appearance of obedience is more important than that which is obeyed, or that which is to be obeyed. By analogy, it is akin to ignoring the word "junk" in the phrase "junk bonds", believing the word "bond" to cancel out the concept behind "junk," which actually gives meaning to the entire phrase. In the same way, the ***appearance of obedience*** not only negates the concept of "obedience"–or, what is really being touted by the parents here, "blind–obedience"—but the methods, meaning, and ideas embodied by the growth-word, ***"discipline,"*** itself.

In my years of coaching, I saw many parents react with the same level of psychological violence toward a child sticking a pin into an electrical socket, as they did when that same child did not respond immediately to be called by name. The parental need for "obedience"–as opposed to the administration of proper discipline–was obvious. Beside the parental demand for obedience however, society and many religions also demand obedience for its own sake. Any breach in the obedience-demand process regardless of the authority demanding it, requires punishment, itself a moral issue, based upon the more powerful, social, cultural, and religious definitions of "good" and "bad."

Discipline neither requires the use of punishment, nor relies upon it as one of its methods of enforcement. It is as we defined it to be earlier: training which perfects, molds, or corrects. It is a learning process that teaches the Principle of Causality that lies behind all life and all human actions: that events have consequences, and that those consequences are consistent with–and are a function of–the causes and effects underlying any and all conditions.

There is no need to call Johnny a "stupid fool," or to break his toys because he sticks a pin into the electrical socket. Granted, the child has to be *taught*. It must *learn*. But this disciplining process–in which teaching and learning become the effective tools of growth–can be accomplished–in this common instance–by the parent either buying childproof plug guards, or simply saying "No" while shaking his or her head. Either action will do. True, it may be necessary for you to repeat yourself fifty times or more before Johnny gets the message. But realistically speaking, repetition is not the issue. The important matter–and what you must pause to ask yourself–is, *"What message do I want Johnny to receive?"*

There is another consideration that requires redefinition and a new understanding in dealing with the concept of child abuse.

Typically, when we think of child abuse, we think strictly in terms of physical abuse. At other times, we may also invoke images of sexual abuse. While these two forms of abuse cannot be overlooked–we must realize there are other forms of psychic cruelty and ego-diminishment that are much more common; and in fact, these other forms are so prevalent, that for all intent and purposes we automatically regard them as "normal." Such oppressive social toleration and cultural views are actually grounded in a universal belief that these "other" forms of abuse actually serve a "useful" purpose. That is, they are unconsciously evaluated as being a "necessary" component of "normal" child rearing, and thus are either ignored, or tolerated without a second thought.

What might such a useful purpose be? Surprisingly, it is one of an impersonal nature, but which is instinctively recognized as being at the root of daily life: the holding on to, and maintenance of, a socialization process which–we contend–is, in fact, dying.

Let us be clear as to what we mean here. In this instance, we postulate that those "other" forms of abuse which are so eagerly and universally tolerated, actually consist of socially induced attitudes–along with their attendant actions or lack of them–that are seen as part of the socialization process, but which are found to be necessary expediencies only in early agricultural communities and assembly line societies. That is, those attitudes and actions that are deemed as necessary in order to instill unthinking diligence, blind attention to detail, and constant self–sacrifice "for the good of all." We see these blindly enforced forms of discipline as forms of abuse which–in the end–not only destroy the psychic vibrancy and flowering brilliance of talented individuals within that social structure, but which end up corroding the very society that has fostered these forms of abuse. In short, we feel that when the agricultural and assembly line phase of any society have evolved past the point of pure survival, the continuation of these forms of enforced behavior–visited upon the offspring of that society–eventually damn it to an inevitable collapse.

While it is true that such qualities are demanded of any *individual* successful life, it is their conscious, judicious use–which must always involve a reasonable consideration for one's self–that is of paramount consideration. Essentially then, only by nurturing and encouraging individual talents and their expression in a *holistic* way, can society not simply "survive," but grow and prosper. It thus becomes clear that the enforcement of positive qualities at the expense of individual integrity, intelligence, and wholesome self-interest, not only constitutes a form of abuse, but produces individuals who are incapable of functioning in a more advanced society–the type of society we have produced today; one that is based upon service and high technology.

Consequently, if we are unwilling or incapable of changing the way we think of ourselves and our children for humanitarian reasons, then the time will most certainly come when we will be forced make these changes out of pure economic necessity. And indeed, if we cannot effect such changes even at that eleventh hour; if the tide of opportunity for equitable change passes us by, then the inevitable conclusion will befall us–both individually and collectively; socially, and economically. It is as simple as that. And the blatantly clear signs of our failure to implement such healthy change up to this point in time, are clearly all around us. In our opinion, the present day state of the of the child abuse and neglect issue is–analogically and comparably speaking–at the level of understanding of heart disease held by 18th century medicine. Some individuals think this comparison is too optimistic. Others regard us as pessimistic. We regard it as all too accurate.

Additionally, it must be recognized and made quite clear, that those social elements interested in the child abuse/neglect issue, are fighting at uphill battle. And the main forms of opposition against which they are struggling are such old bugaboos as the stale, orthodox, non–functional accepted dogmas of psychopathology, "cults," "working mothers" and those two most favorite catchalls, "poverty" and the excuse of "minorities," all of which are seen as the *limiting* causes behind the effective treatment of child abuse. Indeed, modern researchers and clinicians are finding out that these forms of opposition are actually self-serving cultural screens; shields used to mask the complexities and structural elements of the issue, in order to perpetuate and preserve the "status quo"–a social model which has obviously failed.

Yet supporters of the status quo persist, and for no other reason than the status quo, quite simply–that which they know, understand, and can manipulate according to their individual and collective (group) preferences. It is our belief that in the coming decades, child abuse and neglect will be seen for what they are: problems of global proportion that know little class, and which are virtually without religious preference or personality boundaries. Rather, these blights upon society will be recognized for what they are–both individually and group generated, socially dictated social traumas, rooted in the fabric of the socialization process itself.

A Kinder and Gentler Nation Begins
With Caring Treatment of Our Children

The meaning of the above section heading is simple:

1. Society is wholly responsible for the abuse and neglect of its children

2. It is society that determines the types of individuals it will produce to fulfill its explicit and implicit cultural requirements

3. It is society that not only determines the type of individuals who will either perpetuate, modify, or change its purposes and values, but the type of people who will also determine the directions those truths will take

Statements of the obvious? It may appear so at first, until we examine the underlying issues more closely.

First of all, the reader must remember that children have no control over the circumstances into which they are born. They are thus helpless to defend themselves from parents, the influences of others, the values of that society, and that society's institutions. Put bluntly, whatever authorities say to children, they believe.

This situation is further complicated by the fact that in our present day culture, the general value system is one of; sexist individualism, strict ego-aggrandizement without plan, purpose, or concern for personal consequences, interpersonal competitiveness, and blind obedience to authority (in the latter instance, the U.S. Supreme Court's ruling–which upholds and sanctions the use of corporal punishment–presents a public posture that reflects Biblical and early Puritanical America attitudes. That is, we see this ruling as a consciously designed expediency, generated by the political status quo, in order to shore up a failed system of laws and their enforcements, as is evidenced by our society's massive crime problem and its well-known label of "The Murder Capitol of the World." The ruling's stated purpose however, that of being a "necessary" governmental action meant to "deter" threats to the lives of its citizenry, is a further indictment of the failure of our social system. A system that–we contend–has its roots in how we rear and train our young.)

It does not take much of an imagination to see that such high court rulings both support and invest parents with a myriad of additional unspoken and unwritten "freedoms" in their "training" of future producers, consumers and competitors–not to mention the continuation of the "schizoid" socialization process that such dictates further. An important aspect of this "schizoid" socialization process is its imposition on altruism. At some point in their history, all civilizations are judged by how well they care for the weakest and most helpless members of their social structure and how they treat animals (this is typically the point of view held by the news media when it compares the actual behavior of individuals to the accepted regimen of societal, behavioral requirements.) While altruism is all too often one of a culture's proffered positions–as in the case of America–it takes but little scrutiny to see that the more primary and fundamental impulse underlying this "altruism" is actually that of fostering an attitude that one must "win at all costs." Such a secreted view requires individuals who can hold up to extreme competition, learn to become masters of deceit, and have the ability to be merciless–within, of course, the "accepted" guidelines of that society. Thus, while the shouted-from-the-rooftops societal value is that of reducing human suffering, the actual hidden or "nested" value being encouraged is that of becoming "someone,"; of winning at all costs; and of being successful, regardless of the human or environmental consequences.

Is it any wonder then, that our entire repertoire of child rearing practices, and our educational system as a whole, is designed to teach our children how to hate? Because it most certainly requires a venomous hatred to "win at all costs"; and a skillful, well-designed, taught set of "social skills." Social skills that effectively couch the activities needed to produce that "winning attitude" under the guise of "altruistic" behaviors; behaviors that are deemed as "necessary" for "the good of all concerned." And of course, this set of complex mental and social theatrics is executed and encouraged in such a way, that the individual, successful in their application, is hailed as the "Man" or "Woman of the Year." Of course, this subsequent reward is essential if the process is to work. But if one dares to speak the truth about what the system actually teaches; or if one has the temerity to write against the status quo and its social "norms," then it is clear "proof" that the particular "rabble rouser" has simply not been "properly socialized." That is, in the eyes of those unthinking, robotic-mind individuals who unquestioningly support that system of government and its attendant society. For it must be remembered, that "keeping up appearances" is essential for the maintenance and perpetuation of any "system" of government, its society, and hence the very lives of its citizenry. And of course, this includes our own. Thus, we are taught behaviors without conviction or feeling. Is it any wonder that we find it difficult if not virtually impossible to love one another, when we are taught from the very outset that everyone else is clawing their way to the top, and that we are fair game in that ascent?

It is a sad but true fact, that from the moment children are born, they are *taught* the concept of "alienation." This principle of unfriendliness soon becomes their guiding beacon; a measure which they immediately interpret as a life skill necessary for their survival in what they are led to believe is a hostile society, a mixed culture, and a dangerous world-at-large. In imparting this "protective attitude" to them, it is clear that we are not interested in what *they* feel or think. What we are interested in is *what* they say, and in *how* they behave. That is, in what we, ourselves, have come to accept as the "social norm"–an appearance-product-image based facade which denies the inner qualities–the Eternal Verities themselves–as important.

How does this "left-handed" technique work? Through two disjointed–yet complimentary–ploys. First, children are *taught* not to lie. But if they tell the truth about what they see, feel, or think, they are punished. So our children learn to "tell the truth"–that is, they learn to repeat the accepted "party line." Second, and at the same time, they quickly "sense" that they are given tacit permission to figure out ways around "the truth" in order to gain additional parental and societal favor. Why do they need more approval? Because a life based upon lies and self-delusion is never secure–enough is never "enough." In short, then, our children thus learn early on, that what parents and educators *want*, is not what they *say* they want. This bizarre construct–this ineffective, dangerous model of being and behavior–inevitably and rapidly spreads into the deepest recesses of their own mental and emotional worlds, until they do not even know what they are feeling, thinking, seeing, or sensing for *themselves*. It is then but a short step from here; a single movement of the mind, through which they lose themselves within their own fabricated "factory of illusion." They are no longer "who" they "are." They are *what* daddy, mommy, and society tell them they *must* be, in order to survive, win and "prosper."

Why does all of this occur? The answer is surprisingly simple, if not obvious. And that is, because in America, conflict is sewn into the very fabric of society. Not only children, but adults–the very teachers of our children–are torn between the behavioral model extremes of Puritanism and over indulgence. According to numerous anthropologists and social psychologists, this is a result of teaching conflicting values. Let us take an example.

The practice of thrift is seen as a virtue, and is generally taught to the young as an important element of living which should–at the very least–occupy some important position in their life model. On the other hand, the children are also constantly exposed to the desirability and socially proclaimed "need" to drive new cars, have stylish or "designer" clothing and shoes, living in large expensive homes, taking luxurious vacations, and–in general–engaging in all of the activities required to "keep up with the Jones." This, in order to be labeled as "acceptable" members of society. The implementation of these conflicting teachings and demands results in a highly leveraged economy were newscasters and governments alike can speak of "junk bonds" and high social values in the same breath.

Perhaps another common example is called for at this point in order to drive our point home–hard. Children are rigorously taught the importance of the work ethic. We teach them that it is a "fact of life" that if they want to "get ahead" in the world, they must "keep their noses to the grindstone." Yet, all around them they plainly see that the most successful people never seem to work. In fact, they come to think that the most successful individuals are those that are valued for their physical appearance, their social skills and their business contacts, all of which give them the "good life" without diligently applying themselves to the "daily grind." You can see how the problem of American hypocrisy has degraded our society, and all but completely destroyed our most priceless asset–the children.

And there is only one possible conclusion that such diametrically opposed behavior–belief systems can yield. One that may not be apparent at first, but which is nevertheless inevitable. And that is, that we are living for the future, while depleting our natural, intellectual, economic, and essential moral resources in the present, of *both* our adults *and* our children.

Further results stemming from our American system of conflict, confusion, and its attendant behavioral decay, can also be seen in our attitude taken toward those tens of thousands of older people who lose their savings as a direct result of the our country's miasmatic morality; a "con artist" morality is allowed to exist and even flourish. Yet, in the end, these losses are either directly or indirectly repaid–in one form or another–through enforced taxpayer measures; a true reflection of our country's bizarre mixture of fierce competitiveness and altruism. And while the taxpayer must pay for this "altruistic" government act, you will note that the actual culprits responsible for the losses are rarely punished to the degree that their crime warrants. Why is this so? Once again, a little scrutiny of the issue on the part of the reader will reveal the simple truth behind this phenomenon. And that is, that such thievery/replacement/punishment–repeat-the-cycle process, is an activity necessary to insure the survival of the "value system" and the "socialization process" that supports it. It is seen by those in political, social, and economic power–at whatever level–as an expediency needed to maintain momentum in the direction they have determined society should move.

It does not take much of an application of the principles of inductive logic–and common sense–to understand that the only way a culture such as this can function and sleep at night, is through denial. And in the case of American society, that denial has been honed to a very fine, dangerously sharp, razor's edge.

Why do we say this? Why do we think "denial" is the pivot upon which such actions and attitudes can safely oscillate, and in a "balanced" way? One has only to compare the actions sanctioned by the official party line–be that in whatever aspect of society being investigated–and compare those actions to the behavior that takes place off the public screen, to see why no other force can be the responsible agent for this dilemma. Interestingly enough, it is the act of denial that is the first and most primary mechanism underlying all addictions, and the first which must be removed if the addict is to recover.

The sad fact is, that America is a sexist, violent, schizophrenic society, the underlying forces of which are mirrored in such commonalities as our inability to touch or be touched, and to exhibit loving and spontaneous behaviors in both public–as well as private–social interactions. This lack of love and care; this inability to communicate a tenderness and concern through simple human touch; these genuine human values, are abundantly reflected in our treatment of the young and old–both of which are the less productive and more consumptive members of society and its social groups. Other "weak" and "less capable" groups also includes females in general, who–according to a patriarchal belief scheme–require "protection." Yet it is interesting to note, that females are considered to be the primary abusers of children. This *statistical fact* lies in direct contradiction to both matriarchal myth and fact, in which the female is seen as Goddess, nurturer, and protector of the tribe in general, and of children in particular. (It appears that when the world shifted from the maternal Goddess image to the paternal God-image, a time some claim to be a result of males finding out how children were created, the role of the female drastically changed.)

In this force-centered, aggression-laden paternal God-image society, women became chattel. Why did this occur? We see this shift taking place due to the natural male proclivity involved in the general force-aggression theme: the male's *biological need to own things*. Whether this act of "owning" is for a tract of land, a piece of clothing, a weapon, a place to live or as it applies to a human being, it is all the same to the male mentality in such a paternally-driven society. And the direction this need took in terms of immediate availability when it came to "owning" a human being was, of course, the female with whom he lived. Almost over night, from protector and nurturer, she was cast into the role of property; property that had no human rights. Her existence was reduced to one of caring for the male's (other) property, *his* home and *his* children. The females role in the home was viewed as "necessary." That is, as an essential piece of property whose primary purpose was to see to it that the male's sexual desires were satisfied, and to act as a loyal servant who insured that the male's will was cared out in his absence.

In modern times, the well-meaning attempt to liberate women from this role has utterly failed. The panacea for such liberation has become that of casting her into the role of a "breadwinner"; the role (until recently) reserved exclusively for the male. She has been goaded into becoming a fighter; a warrior, every bit as battle-hardened and embittered as her male counterpart, in clawing her way to the top of the business, academic, sports, or any other world one cares to name. Of course, it is a fact that females can and most certainly do function as bread winners. Thus, their coming "into their own" in terms of sharing economic power with the male is clearly *one* way in which these (former) "slaves" can be liberated. However, for them to become "carbon copies" of males in terms of their attitudes toward life and nature, is to extinguish all hope of their flowering as human beings, while offering the more cooperative, compassionate, and gentler roles which only their gender can naturally and biologically provide within the family of the human species.

The brutality of the socially enforced model of the "contemporary female breadwinner" has placed many women–particularly those of the lower classes who have been left in the position of being both mother and bread winner–in a confused, angry, and hopeless state. And their resulting frustration, rejection, and contempt for the system at large, coupled with their lack of respect for other competing females in general, has produced an army of "phantom people," one in which its "soldiers" neither know their current social roles, understand the ones they have been led into, nor know how to flow effortlessly into that mold which American society has dictated they should flow. It is no wonder that "statistics" reflect female violence toward the more helpless and needy–their own, or others'–children.

Any yet, it is statistical analyses such as these that often mislead researchers into thinking that increased female work-activity in the business, professional worlds will–*"must"*–result in increased economic benefit the likes of which will most assuredly remedy the personal life-conditions under which these women are laboring. When these same researchers and their field component–the social workers–come to find that the wealthy abuse their children as equally as do the middle classes, they are horrified. But since the status quo; the accepted "norms" of this distorted, conflicting, morally decaying American system of anti-values is all they know, they refuse to make the logical move into examining the doctrines and dogmas upon which the "norm" itself is based. Even though they recognize that incidents of child abuse by the wealthy are rarely reported–owing to their power and status–and that the absence of such data effects their own statistical analyses, they rationalize away such "loose data" as they term it, and continue on as before, complicating the underlying social problems, and obscuring the reasons for those problems, even further.

But even this is not enough for them. These same researchers, health professionals, and social workers skew their own data still further, when they engage in that mind set and its behavioral carry-through that is so well known in all social sciences circles. Specifically, we are referring to the fact that there are but few physicians, family therapists, and psychologists at best, who report suspected child abuse when it involves children of their "peers." Yet these same individuals exhibit "professional" behavior with great zeal and readiness, when it comes to reporting their concerns of abuse as the relate to children of the middle and lower classes. Of course, the reader can clearly see and understand the implication of such socially-induced, prejudicial, professionally "courteous" conduct.

As we have indicated, it is our belief that child abuse is fundamentally embedded in our social structure due to the patriarchal value system. We therefore hold that child abuse is a function of our intrinsic belief structure, and the socialization processes that supports such a structure. This primary form of socialization is not simply skill oriented; but rather, regulatory in nature. Our arguments in this regard, are that the specific form of regulation taught, is a function of class and culture as a whole, coupled to the economic model in place at the time– be it that of the hunter-gather, the agriculturist, the assembly line worker, the service standard, or the high-tech designer or industrialist. In terms of child abuse as it appears within our own social motif, these "regulatory" measures are violent in nature, and are themselves the inevitable outgrowths of the socialization-belief system itself: spanking, slapping, and hitting. In the initial stages of child rearing, such "regulators" serve as the mechanism of primary reinforcement, only to be replaced at a later time–as the child grows older and is better able to understand and comprehend language–by a secondary, "carry-through" process of regulation that is extremely effective and long-lived: that of verbal violence (and in point of fact, this phase lasts throughout the child's lifetime, owing to its effective use by society at large.) But regardless of whether the violence is physical, sexual or verbal, the result is the same: a fundamentally rigid, passively hostile, fearful personality, which fits well into our economic model and culture "spirit."

Verbal Violence, Threat to Damage, Threat to Withdraw Love and Protection
(The great hidden sin)
Threats of Supernatural Punishment, Are All Crimes

Leaving violent physical and sexual abusive behavior behind for a moment, we are forced to conclude that verbal violence–this secondary "carry-through" process of regulation–is the primary method we use in "educating" our children; this, in order to "fit" them into specific cultural categories that we–that is, society-at- large–have predetermined for them. Essentially, verbal violence in America is used in child rearing as a means by which a child is intimidated by the threat of some form of impending harm, or by the promise of a threat in which some physical or psychological need such as food, or parental love and protection–is threatened to be removed or withheld. In the latter case, the threat of withdrawal of essential love and protection is similar in content and composition to the threats used by every religion in establishing dominance and control over their believers. It is a sophisticated form of intimidation that becomes the central dogma of these institutions, as they develop their creeds, and become more sophisticated in administering to their members. Once again, we can see the interplay between the various sets of society. Relative to child rearing however, we can understand how the threat of violence or of the removal of protection and love, rapidly instill in the child a sense of worthlessness, uselessness, and chronic psychic tension, all of which are more difficult to treat then the more obvious forms of physical and sexual abuse.

We as a society have agreed–at least in a public way–that physical and sexual abuse must cease. But in fact, we have not yet identified or recognized that abuse designed to cause fear and pain by threatening the withdrawal of love, is often much, much more devastating. Why have we failed in this recognition? Because it is so common.

Parents who use the withdrawal of love and support in coercing a child into "behaving," are committing child abuse.

Parents who use the withdrawal of love and support in coercing a child into "behaving," *are* committing child abuse;

abuse that is in every sense as real; in every sense as powerful in its effects upon the child, as are those corporeal measures used by a parent who physically beats his or her child. These verbally abusive individuals require treatment and re-education in a similar way, just as those physically violent parents require other forms of treatment, in addition to the obvious intervention.

But the way we treat children in our beloved American "super" society is necessary; it is seen and held as a requirement in the deepest levels of our unconscious and psychological strata, in order for us to have a class to exploit, and this, by a still smaller class which does the exploiting. This smaller class is reminiscent of the early priest and kingly class so well represented in the Bible and early society. It is based on linear, competitive hierarchy with a the most powerful Alpha male on top.

**Chapter 4
Abuse vs. Neglect**

While neglect is a very important component in the entire abuse-process, our focus will primarily be on the active elements of that process. For the sake of argument, we will differentiate abuse from neglect by making use of the concepts of "Commission" and "Omission." While there are exceptions to this differentiation, we feel that it will nonetheless be useful for descriptive or qualitative purposes.

To begin. If you will note, most researchers are looking for the reasons or causes underlying the child abuse issue. Yet few researchers have dared to approach the issue from another angle. An angle that begins by asking the question, "Why should parents *not* abuse their children?" Of course, the approach to the problem is outright rejected if it is mentioned. Why is it summarily dismissed out-of-hand? We advocate that the reason for this rejection is due to the self-delusional morality of American society; a morality that openly and indignantly professes its concerned for "human rights." As such, the idea of entertaining such a line of questioning would admit to the universal existence of child abuse within the same society that is proclaiming its concern for human welfare! But as we have seen, the American model is deeply entrenched in the idea of chattel. And all chattel–that is, "property- owing"–models require abuse in one form or another, both to ensure the effective working of that model, as well as to perpetuate it. So why should this new avenue of questioning not be explored? The answer of course, is that is *should* be *seriously* undertaken. In reality however, we are confident that it will be continuously rejected, owing to the basic propositions of the chattel model itself.

Nevertheless, we have asked this question in the past, and persist in doing so to this day, as unsavory as it may seem. In those instances when we asked it, we usually received the following answers from parents and clinicians– that is, after they have recovered from the initial shock of the asking of this question in the first place. The spectrum of their answers included:

Because:
Parents love their children.
They are theirs.
They are small and helpless
It's not right.
It's against God law.
It's against society.
It's against the law.
It's against nature.
It's awful.
It's just not right.
I'd never think of such a thing.
They can't fight back.

It does not take a specialist in psychopathology or psychiatry to see that these answers provide little in the way of information. Instead, they focus on media "truisms" (hype–the going, accepted, social "line") and upon vagaries that are meant to justify a national, moral, quasi-religious stance. A stance anchored in the "obvious" differences between the concepts of Good and Evil, Right and Wrong, Innocence and Guilt. These nebulous ramblings–the results of a peoples' social miasma and their ensuing refusal in dealing with empirical reality–*allow* people to abuse people, regardless of what ideals, prohibitions or injunctions to which they posture they hold so dear. Yet even here, these same individuals will admit that there is something especially awful about abusing someone who is helpless, dependent, and who is the "…flesh or my flesh." Abuse of the helpless then, even to the most hardened of society, seems to violate the intrinsic belief that children are one of God's most precious gifts, and should be treated with love, respect and kindness. The convolutions of the dilemma, are therefore without bounds.

In keeping with the "spirit" of this twisted predicament, attempts are made by the establishment to explain away abuse by focusing on variables that do not directly threaten the present authority and power structure. It takes but little analysis on the part of the reader to realize that such "explanations"–actually and in fact–reinforce and stabilize the overall force of authority and its operations that lie behind the power structure. These variables include working mothers, the poor, minorities, females–and psychopathology itself.

While animal analogs do not prove much in relating their behavior to human child abuse issues, they are, nevertheless, quite suggestive. Animals do not abuse their offspring. However, they do kill them under certain circumstances, these circumstances being severe injury, weakness, over crowding, food shortage, and spousal "displacement." It is curious to note that there is some evidence humans have engaged in similar behavior. For instance, entire cultures are known to have murdered female infants, destroyed children with birth defects, practiced cannibalism on their young, and tolerated the killing of infants by males when those infants competed for the female's time and attention. While these cultures are regarded as primitive and savage by modern and Western social standards, it must be admitted that such extreme behavior has a rationale basis–given the times and circumstances of their commission–as compared to the often senseless brutalities of physical and emotional violence perpetrated and *perpetuated*, in so-called "enlightened" and "civilized" Western countries.

Of what survival values do such actions as, for example, tying a child to a bed and burning it with hot pokers, or forcing the child to perform fellatio with the genetic father and then damning it to hell, serve? We might manage an intellectual and emotional escape from such episodes of senseless brutality if they were rare. We might even effect such escapes from them by labeling the father as pathologic, and one who is simply in need of treatment. But as the seemingly endless barrage of recent television Real Crime Shows have shown, such brutality is not only more prevalent than suspected–or admitted to?–but in most cases, the adult responsible for inflicting such treatment has always been considered by his peers to be an upstanding citizen and "bastion" of the community. The tragic fact which we are finding out, is that secret cruelties and tortures are *not* "rare" in our "civilized" American culture.

How do we, then, make our escape from the less graphic and horrible brutalities? By what means do we break free of the subtler forms of child torture and denigration? Actually, as a society, we are quite good at it. Our ability in this area of socialization has been unconsciously constructed and ordered through a complex process that begins with an infinite level of justification, shorn up by incessant self-delusion, and "perfectly" rounded out with internal rationalizations. More to the point, we escape from them by convincing ourselves that such treatments are socially acceptable. How can this be? Easy! They have history and folk wisdom to support them! After all, they are the "traditional" means of raising children in the "right" way, so that they become "Good, God-fearing American citizens." More importantly, for some individuals, such measures of child "rearing" are actually believed to be necessary moral treatments for the survival of the species!

Just what are some of these less graphic, subtle, but tremendously damning child brutalities that are so common, we regard them as normal and necessary if our society is to grow and flourish? To name but a few, we have: washing the mouth out with soap, forced enemas, dragging, hair pulling, arm yanking, face slapping, hitting, humiliating, embarrassing, sensory deprivation, spanking, metaphysical damnation (threat–"God will send you to Hell if you don't do what daddy and mommy say!") name calling, labeling (Incompetent label–"You're stupid!" Failure label–"You'll never amount to anything!"), defining ("You don't have the ability to do that" or, "You're no good with your hands!"), screaming, yelling and so on. The list is endless. While these do not appear to be as horrible at face value when compared to the extreme cases of physical brutality we mentioned above, have you ever looked into a child's face–and especially into the windows of its soul–its eyes–when confronted by these behaviors? For if you do; if you pay at some–not even close–attention, you will see the presence of utter rejection in its expression, and literally, terror in its eyes. And why should the child not exhibit these negative, physical projections? After all, it has been hurled into the black, bottomless pit of helpless terror and confusion: an insensible state; one enormously magnified by further feelings of worthlessness and abandonment, these latter disturbances being a secondary emotional set that stem from a primary perception of being completely unloved.

Why helpless? Simply because there is nothing he or she can do about it. Why terrified? Because the child's imagination builds the situation into an almost death experience. Why confused? The young one cannot believe that someone it trusted; someone it needs and depends upon, has turned on it with such apparent frenzy. (If the reader would like to test the validity of these premises, all they need to do is spend an afternoon in their local supermarket or mall.) Hence, the child *must* conclude that something is wrong with it. This is the first–and only–conclusion it can draw. Further, if this more subtle violence is committed upon the child at too early an age, the child will most probably come to accept–and literally expect–such demeaning treatment to be both normal and natural. And you can be certain it will carry these proclivities into the next generation, by visiting them upon its own children. For the individual will come to see such treatment as a "normal" way of rearing its own offspring. And why not? After all, this is the way is was raised, and "...it didn't do me any harm" being the final justification for the perpetuation of this abuse-model. While the author most emphatically acknowledge and outright reject the horror and impact of both physical and sexual abuse, the reader is reminded at this point that the purpose of this book is the exploration of mental, emotional and interpersonal abuse. For we believe, that these are the "hidden abuse and addictions" of a hypocritical American culture–one that says one thing, while doing another.

While such "subtle" forms of abuse are frequently neglected–as we have pointed out–they *are* yet acknowledged by most states as one of the four types of abuse. The reason given for placing less emphasis on mental, interpersonal and emotional abuse (*MIE*), is that it is more difficult to define and even more difficult to legally and clinically observe. But most importantly, the reason it is so universally ignored in American society, is that outside attempts to remedy it are seen as unwanted intrusions that violate the "sanctity" of the American family. And exactly *what* does this phrase, "Sanctity of the American family," really mean? Put succinctly, it means that each male has the right to raise his family as he sees fit. Of course, when statements like this are publicly extolled, we usually hear the stirring music of "America the Beautiful," or the "Star Spangled Banner" playing, while the flag waves; whether this be in some actual physical setting, or in some designed, controlled, dramatic emotional dialogue-event, such as a sermon from the pulpit. At the root of all this pomp and pageantry however, there nevertheless resides one very simple, inevitable meaning: that males socialized in the hierarchical patriarchal process, have the obligation and duty to assure that their children fulfill the roles that *society* has dictated for them. Truly then, a man's home is *not* his castle. It is nothing more than a place in which he performs his acts of violence; and those with the complete sanction of a society that will benefit from those acts. It is our opinion then, that *MIE* is primarily ignored for the latter, more important reason. That is, it is a necessary part of a socialization process which this society has designed, perpetuates, and reinforces daily–as is necessary–in order to produce those types of individuals which this society deems necessary for its continuation.

To put it another way–and to belabor this important point for the reader's benefit–*MIE* is essential for producing the types of individuals a society requires to maintain and perpetuate *its own particular values and world view*. As previously stated, America desires individuals who are independent, highly competitive, and who verbalize altruistic values and ideals, whether they actually believe and follow them or not. This also explains why and how Donald Trump got elected president; as he embodies these exact values and ideals. But at the same time, this country's multidimensional social subculture–coupled with its "single-image" superstructure–demand that these same individuals be completely obedient, unquestioning, and blindly supportive of the principles and dictates of the socialization process itself; It further demands that these individuals give absolute allegiance to the status quo sub and super-system it has also created, which assures such full, blind, support. Truly, in terms of inductive logic, America is founded upon–and operates through–a Circular Argument concept. That is, one in which what is assumed to be true–and which is enforced as being true–is seen to be correct "as is," in and of itself.

It must be remembered, that production and consumption are the highest values held in America. As such, it is necessary to train individuals to meet these cultural requirements, and this of course, is done through the socialization process. The type of individuals this culture desires then, are the rigid authoritarian male-types, and passive hysterical-females types. As women continue to enter the work force, they too are being required to become as rigid and authoritarian as their male counterparts, if they are to successfully compete with men for power, prestige and positions of leadership. And as every reader is no doubt aware, this trend can now be observed in women becoming every bit as "tough" and unfeeling as their male counterparts. In our opinion, this will only lead to more and greater *MIE* in the years ahead.

FORMS OF ABUSE
Five Primary Abuse Modes Are

All forms of child abuse interfere with the healthy and creative functioning of the child. Abuse of any kind handicaps the individual in one or more important areas of development, while at the same time, over emphasizes attributes that properly belong to other areas of psychic development. It must be remembered, that it is absolutely impossible for the primary form of abuse–whether it be physical, emotional, mental, sexual or interpersonal–not to inhibit functioning in other areas of the child's life.

Abused children have the highest rates of developmental problems, incidents of juvenile delinquent behavior, and, as adults, show the highest incidence of addictions. The latter include addiction to food, alcohol, sex and drugs. They also have the highest rate of psychopathological disturbances, in addition to exhibiting the highest rate of criminal behavior.

And not surprisingly, they also have the highest probability of becoming child abusers themselves.

Physical abuse interferes with:
1. emotional
2. mental
3. sexual
4. interpersonal
5. physical

Emotional abuse interferes with:
1. mental
2. sexual
3. interpersonal
4. physical
5. emotional

Mental abuse interferes with:
1. emotional
2. sexual
3. interpersonal
4. physical
5. mental
6. development

Interpersonal abuse interferes with:
1. emotional
2. interpersonal
3. physical
4. mental
5. sexual

Sexual abuse interferes with:
1. emotional
2. mental
3. physical
4. sexual
5. interpersonal

Premise: Physical Abuse Is

1. The use of initiatory violence to enforce one's will upon the child
2. Retaliating with violence toward a child's behavior. Such types of retaliation include, but are not limited to: throwing objects, pushing, shoving, pinching and grabbing, slapping, spanking, kicking, biting, throwing, beating, threatening with a gun, knife or other object; using an external object to inflict damage; burning, drowning, forcing, locking the child up in closet, and violent force feeding.

Premise: Mental Abuse Is

1. The teaching of irrational and illogical points of view as *the* standard to be used in the identification and solution of life problems and or challenges. For example, the belief in the infallibility of authority; justifying violence by calling it discipline; invoking God as overseer and final punisher for "bad" behavior.
2. Creating "absolute" models of behavior. Example. "Now just look at Johnny! He's how a boy *should* be! I wish he was *my* son!"
3. Frequent use of such absolute terms such as, "always," and "never," etc.
4. The teaching of morality through dictatorial attitudes and by lecturing, rather than through setting positive examples for the child to imitate. Such positive examples would include the parent's equitable actions toward, and treatment of, him/her self and others.
5. The making of metaphysical statements concerning the inherent "good" or "evil" nature of the child, or such nature(s) as it (they) may apply to others.

6. Teaching ideas through fear.

7. Teaching parental beliefs, ideas, and values before the child develops the critical reasoning faculty needed to evaluate and estimate the validity of those beliefs, ideas, and values for him or herself.

8. Being overly preoccupied with the future and the past.

9. Providing inappropriate information as a function of context or developmental level. This includes insulting the child's intelligence, and providing too much data.

Premise: Emotional Abuse Is

1. Creating fear in the child through yelling, name calling, threats of abandonment, violence, or institutionalization.

2. Humiliating or embarrassing the child in public or private.

3. Blaming the child for the parent's problems.

4. Defining a script for the child to follow in either their actions or their play. Example. "You should play nice, like your sister," or "You are so much like your grandfather or grandmother."

5. Forcing the child to be something it doesn't want to be, and then justifying it by claiming that it is for the child's own good.

6. Defining what is possible and what is not possible for the child to accomplish in the future.

7. Making statements such as, "You're no good, everything you do is wrong!" Or such negative declarations as, "You'll will wind up in jail, or on the street," "You're a whore, a drunk" etc. (We call this "Prophesying." Parents frequently use this technique when they are frustrated with their own lives and feel powerless.)

Premise: Interpersonal Abuse Is

1. Forcing a child to make, or the making of alliances with a parent, such that one adult is favored over another. It is the witnessing of verbal abusive behavior between two adults that generally sets the tone for this alliance.
2. Displaying differential treatment for similar acts between siblings.
3. Humiliating one sibling in front of another.
4. Making one sibling morally responsible for another.
5. Using the successes or failures of one sibling to influence or control another.

Premise: Sexual Abuse Is

1. The forcing or coercion of children to engage in adult sexual activity.
2. Forcing a child to witness adult sexual activity
3. Adult manipulation of the genitals as the primary focus of the adult providing "care" for the child. This occurs through such mundane acts as changing diapers, giving baths, or tending to wounds, etc. Also, those physical actions disguised for the purpose of genital play, viewing, or/and manipulation.

Premise: What Is Not Abusive Behavior

1. Physical Behavior: grabbing a child to prevent it from harming itself, another person, or property.
2. Emotional Behavior: raising your voice to stop behavior which is inappropriate to a situation. (In such an instance, this measure is typically used to gain the child's attention.)
3. Mental Behavior: saying "yes," "no," or "maybe," as is appropriate for a specific situation, in order to provide the child with qualified information.

4. Interpersonal Behavior: allowing the child to model adult and others' behavior in order to learn new skills.

5. Sexual Behavior: discussing sex and procreation from an intelligent, knowledgeable, and rational point of view. The sharing of an adult's positive feelings about sex and sexual relationships in general.

Patterns of Abusive Behavior
Pattern Number 1

Parent Type–Mother. Dependent, rejecting, overprotective and domineering. She controls the home, but is fearful of her position.

Parent Type–Father. Authoritarian and inadequate. He will display petty bureaucratic tendencies, and have a dislike and actual fear of the child. If the child is male, he will display a strong resentment toward it. If the child is female, he will possibly indulge in sexual abuse with the child, or/and make alliances with it.

Child Recipient–If a female, she will regard herself and others as Superior. If the child is a male, he will regard himself and others as inferior, but also see himself as a necessary "evil." That is, as an individual whose role is expressly designed for earning money and for breeding purposes. Ironically, a male in such a family may also develop high aspirations and be possessive, while a female will be possessive and have low aspirations.

This particular pattern also leads to children who become drug, alcohol and food abusers, as well as over- achievers.

Pattern Number 2

Parent Type–Father. Authoritarian. Adequate in worldly matters. A high achiever. Fearful of showing his feelings, very fearful of failure. Normally this type of father will raise an hysterical-type daughter, and a son whom he sees as "...not living up to snuff." He may be a heavy consumer of alcohol. Such a father-type also exhibits a tendency to emotional outbursts.

Parent Type–Mother. She is passive, dependent and submissive. She rarely drinks but rather, suffers in silence, or manipulates the dominant father through passive- aggressive means or through sexual maneuvers.

Child Recipients–If a male, he will be regarded by self and others as being superior. If female, she will be regarded by self and others being inferior. Further, she will see herself as a necessary "evil" meant exclusively for breeding and child care.

Pattern Number 3

Mother–Fearful, childish, easily hurt, and needy. She is compliant in most matters. She snipes at the weaknesses of the husband. She tends to form alliances against the father with female children. All attempts to exert her authority are undifferentiated and ineffective. Uses guilt and martyrdom as control devices. She will engage in viscous verbal, abusive attacks during times of weakness. She is the dependent type, and exhibits fundamentally cold and non-supportive behavior. She is also fearful of the child/children growing up, and extremely jealous of her offspring(s) successes.

Father–Passively authoritarian and lazy. He has high aspirations and ideals, but exerts little effort in manifesting their achievement. He is either a "Wanna be..." or "Could have been" type. In general, he is indifferent towards his children and those of others. When he does become involved with his offspring, he tends to be moralistic. As stated before, he is primarily not interested in his own children.

Child Recipient–The male offspring of this parent-set type set is generally regarded by others as being superior. His own views of himself can be grandiose, leading to an arrogance that can get out of hand. Generally, however, he is capable of fulfilling his superior self-image generated dreams, at least to some reasonable degree. He usually treads a somewhat fine line between what is socially and legally acceptable, and what is not. This type of child is seen as an "adult" by other children, as well as by adults.

On the other hand, the female offspring of such parents is typically regarded by others as being inferior. There is no grandiosity or arrogance here. Rather, such a child typically displays a tendency toward playing approved social roles which bring her the acceptance of her peers and adults e.g., Cheerleader, Sports Team Manager, etc.

In effect, this type of female is viewed as being a "nice child," by both her peers and adults in general.

Both male and female children of this parental-type have high anxiety profiles, and tend to abuse alcohol and drugs.

Pattern Number 4

Child Types–Male: Highly dependent and fearful male. Suffers from deep sense of guilt and anxiety.

Child Type–Female: Childlike and fearful. As with the male of this Pattern set, she suffers from guilt and anxiety.

Pattern Number 5

Child Type–Male: Intellectually domineering. Fearful of social disapproval and therefore "plays it safe."

Child Type–Female: Intellectually oriented female.

Has difficulty in showing affection or emotion.

Later, as married adults, such a child-couple are primarily

unfriendly though not hostile toward each other. Such a duo tend to stay together due to social reasons, in addition to their deep seated–but denicd–feelings of dependency, the latter stemming from hidden feelings of inadequacy.

From such a union, both the male and female children that are produced will tend toward intellectualism, but will be ineffectual and emotionally distant to their children, as their parents were to them. Children emerging from this Pattern-type suffer constant criticism from others, in addition to experiencing a high personal demand for success and power.

**The Abused Child Is Not to Blame,
Not Even As An Adult**

Yes, it is true. The abused child is not to blame–not even when it becomes an adult. Why? Ask yourself: If the template of development used to rear the child was one of abuse, how can it possibly grow into anything else? After having been shaped and fashioned in an ineffective, intrinsically negative way by those who reared it, it's reference frames are distorted at best, and so can only yield behaviors that corresponds to its own template-training? Is it any wonder then, that the child–as both a child and later as an adult–frequently becomes an accomplice in his own misery and suffering?

This is one reason why helping an abused child can be so very difficult: the child–through no fault of his own–sees itself as having "benefited" from the abuse. As a consequence–and in fact–the child feels guilty for any gains it may have accumulated in spite of that abuse. Why is this psychic scenario played out thus? Because in the child's mind, no matter what the primary caretakers do–or did–to it, their actions are seen by the child as still being correct in "some way." To think differently is an impossibility for most children. Thus, the child's model of behavior becomes a comfortable one; one in which it identifies with the aggressors themselves, metering out its own self-punishment for acts committed against its loving parental authority. For it must be remembered, that if the child suffers at the hands of its parents, it automatically believes that it is at fault. Thus, such a child sees itself as always being guilty; and it is only in later life that proper therapy can prove them to be–and to have been–innocent, from their earliest years.

"I am your father; I am your mother." These are special status statements which give "rights" to people; "rights" used to violate the fundamental dignities of others without fear of retaliation. In point of fact, this "Special Status Role" (*SSR*) designation should imply knowledge and responsibility only; and not be used as a special set of "rights" to violate the dignity, value or sanctity of another human being.

"What" Is the Parent and "What" Is the Child?

Parenthood creates responsibilities: not rights. No parent has the right to destroy, or attempt to destroy, the dignity and value of its child. So, just *what is* a parent? A parent is a guardian and an educator only. In short, it is an adult who assumes the conscious responsibility for having brought a new, innocent being into existence through the natural act of procreation.

What then, is a child? First off, we can tell you what a child is **not**. It is not the "property" of the parent. A child *is* an autonomous living being that possesses a mind, a will, a nebulous constellation of emotions, and a complex psychic structure of its own. As such, it must be encouraged and developed only in the most loving, life- sustaining, and enhancing ways possible.

All Other Forms of Human Violation Start With Child Abuse

All of our social ills result from our attitude regarding the nature, worth, and "ownership" of our children.

Sooner or later, our attitudes concerning our children will be found to be generalizations of our attitudes about ourselves. It is this internal projection that can be seen throughout human society as, for example, in the government's attitude concerning its citizens; an attitude that is appallingly similar to the attitude most parents take toward their children. If considered, one will find that this attitude possesses a structural basis. And what is the essential structure of this attitude? It consists of a foundation composed of the "classical" Paternal "rights" projection, upon which a punitive demeanor superstructure is then erected. In short, "Do as I say, not as I do, or else it's off to the wood shed with you for a sound thrashing!" **Our very ideas regarding the ills of an abused child are themselves abusive, and actually prevent recovery.**

Chapter 5

Causal Theories

Typical "causal theories" underlying such ideas are found to have the following general properties:

All causal theories–when broken down–are at best, merely descriptive by nature. Lacking hard-core scientific definition, statistical analyses, a quantifiable mathematical rigor along with physically-based, variably-controlled circumstances, such causal theories–themselves take on abusive and dehumanizing qualities.

Psychopathology

This is the most misleading and sometimes the most ridiculous view, particularly in terms of establishing a clear, well-defined, Cause–Effect relationship. In themselves, psychopathological arguments tend to degrade into an overly simplistic view of Cause and Effect, thereby taking on a paternalistic interpretation. In assuming such simplicity, this ultimate interpretation itself becomes glaringly abusive.

What do we mean here? By its own "rules" of application, psychopathology is based on the theory that the "average" represents that which "should be." In other words, if an entire culture battered its women and children as a matter of course, then that culture would view any member who did not batter its children and women as being "pathological."

The psychopathological view is again descriptive when it states the characteristics of child abusers. Since a descriptive statement cannot–by the established rules of inductive logic–have a causal argument-component embedded in it, the very idea of causality in description misleads researchers into drawing erroneous conclusions as to its "effects." Effects which–in themselves–cannot follow from the given "descriptive" premise, i.e., from that initial statement made or implied which has become the very basis for the analysis itself!

If child abuse is indeed more common then we imagine, than the concept of psychopathology would have to be applied to the socialization process in general. And as we know, this would be an inappropriate use of the term, no matter how emotionally satisfying it might be.

Historical, Cyclic Patterns

This concept is based on the, "Monkey see, monkey do" theory. This concept is actually a learning model, and is one description of how abusive behavior is learned and passed on.

Low Socio-Economic Status (SES)

This condition is conveniently–and typically–used to assign blame–that is, becomes the "Cause"–for all social and interpersonal ills. Members of society who fall into this lower socio-economic status (*SES*) group, are thus frequently over-represented in criminal, violent and "social evil studies," for numerous reasons. The middle class and the wealthy generally support this theory, since it focuses the spotlight of social attention on the behavior of this group, while casting the behavior of the middle and wealthy classes in the shadows. The lower class therefore, become the "identified patient," as in psychoanalytical parlance.

Child abuse has no class-structure boundaries. Simply put, pain, humiliation, and a sense of worthlessness, have no class.

It is important to keep in mind that while reported physical abuse is indeed less frequent in the upper classes, in no way does this indicate that such abuse does not occur. A good metaphor for this, is that while a poor person may use a Timex and a rich one a Rolex, both still tell the time. The only difference lies in the social status projected. In the world of hard reality, we have found that the wealthier a person, the more likely he or she is to use forms of mental and emotional abuse in order to inflict their will upon their children; however "Rolex-like" these more sophisticated forms and "abuse-delivery" methods may be.

Stress

By nature, stress is more of an *Effect* than it is a *Cause*. Yet, it must be kept in mind that this phenomenon itself is circular in nature, i.e., the stress reinforces the *Cause*, which then increases the stress (*Effect*).

Religious Motivation

Both traditional, fundamentalists, and "cult" groups have a particular view on "what" humans are, and on "how" they should be treated.

World-Motivated Model

Models are attempts to understand, order, and predict. The knowledge gained from the modeling process, is then used to control events. Models are thus based upon definitions and expectations. They are, of course, selective. That is, in Model Theory, some events are seen as more important than others.

For example. In capitalism, property is seen as being more important than people. In socialism, providing the necessities for people is deemed as being more important than the accumulation of wealth.

Consider the model "God is good, Man is evil," in terms of the child abuse issue. Just how much *"Cause"* and *"Effect"* – that is, how much "justification," does such a model substantiate? Ponder the definitions of "Evil," "God," "Good," along with the expectations inherent in the statement, "God is good, Man is evil."

How much self-fulfilling, anticipation and prophesying does this model encourage, not to mention the myriad of self-fulfilling actions that flow from it, and which can and do lead to child abuse?

What effect does the model, "Children are the property of the parent, the state, or belong to God?" have on child abuse? In America, children are thought to belong to the parent. In the former USSR, they were seen as being the property of the State. In Christianity, Judaism and Islam, they are thought to be the property of God.

What might be the effect of a model that states: "Children are not the property or possession of anyone, save themselves?" What impact could such a model have on the child abuse issue? It's certainly something worth thinking about, isn't it?

What effect does the model, "Spare the rod, spoil the child," have on child abuse?

What effect on child abuse does the model, "By their very nature, children are stupid," have on both children and adults? How many cases of child abuse can be attributed to this single model–concept alone?

What effect does the model, "Survival of the fitness" have on child abuse?

These and other models have often been combined to come up with a multi-causal theory. For example. Combining low *SES* with stress, and then combining this mixture with an "Imitation Model," leads to yet another, more complex theory. Finally, in daily practice, all such theories eventually become interwoven, thus reducing the entire idea of Causality–that is, of established, inductively valid Cause and Effect relationships in a given phenomenon–to one of utter absurdity.

Our point here: searching for "Absolute Causes"–as in a "clearly defined" Cause-Effect relationship–in the typical sense, not only becomes a ridiculous exercise in futility; such an exercise leads to erroneous assumptions and conclusions: specious, incorrect assumptions and conclusions that are evidenced all around the reader in his or her everyday life experience.

Instead, we will assume that Child Abuse is unacceptable *because* we have chosen a *model* which says it is *unacceptable*. Once we accomplish this, we can proceed with methods for preventing child abusive behavior.

It is our belief, that the phenomenon of child abuse leads to almost every other type of social problem, ranging from criminal behavior and alcohol addiction, to stress-related diseases.

Child abuse–although a hot topic of public "concern"– is still treated in a casual manner, when compared to other perceived social difficulties. A drop of four hundred points in the Stock Market on any given day, is given more attention and coordinated, organized, single-minded social action, than are those thousands of children brought into the emergency rooms of hospital across the country on that same day due to abuse, or who hide in a corner, wondering why they are being punished. Why are we so self-righteously callous? Because we–as "Americans"–simply care more for our material property, than we do for our children. It is as damning and complete a reason as that. And it is a just indictment of the culture and social system in which we–as "Americans"–live. Because it is we who have created this so-called "culture" and social system; not some government "out there." *We* are the government–at least we are, according to our own "sacred" Constitution and laws. *We* have no one to blame for that "other" government that–nevertheless–does exist "out there," and which has gotten out of hand as much as it has in all respects, including its ignoring and even fostering child abuse by its parochial attitudes. It is a horrific accusation against the "glory" of our so-called "free- enterprise system" itself, and an indictment of the battle-cry of "human rights for all" that we proffer and posture so very well to the rest of the world.

A culture which fosters child abuse is not only ugly: it is primitive, vindictive, and–in the end–self destructive. This indictment means that the model we–in this American "culture" of ours–use, must undergo a radical change. And to effect such change, requires that those who hold power will have to share it with those that who do not.

But of course, there is a problem with this simple but effective process. And that is, that cultural model(s) are rarely stated explicitly. Again, why? *Because in stating them, we become conscious of the defects both in the socialization process and in ourselves.*

How do we rectify this? By continuously exposing the negative cultural-value elements and beliefs in detail: not simply through some general reference, or in some vague passing way. An example of such a negative cultural element and belief to which we can apply this idea would be that of the Patriarchal Model. Here we would say that since this model dictates: "Women are inferior to men and are owned by men. They are the man's property. Boys are preferable to girls, and children in general are the property of the male. All of this means that men have the certain rights which women and children do not, including the right to be violent and abusive." By thus exposing the details of this–and other–models, in addition to questioning the validity of their operational premises, we have the opportunity to change them to suit a new, more humanistic model. One that is both more accurate in its depiction of the situation, and which also is in more harmonious alignment with the laws of nature.

Another model we can investigate is that of child care. A more humanistic approach to this model requires that we ask ourselves some very important questions. The first being: "How does society's actions, values, goals, and beliefs, enhance or impede the healthy development of children?"

The next logical question might be: "What does the healthy development of children consist of, when we view this question–not from cultural, religious or societal "ideal"–but from a more universal perspective?"

We might better understand this process if we ask ourselves how we would want to be perceived by some external, hypothetical observer, and how we–if we could–might want to remember ourselves after our death, and indeed, how we wish ourselves to be remembered by others after we depart of this life.

We want the reader to be aware that these questions and the others we ask are most definitely biased toward an ideology which supports rationality, research, growth, joy and life challenges–as virtues. In other words, a hunter-gather society, an industrial, agricultural, or techno-bureaucratic society would not have these as goals, and we reject such societies for their both their overt and covert violence, and for their overall human ineffectiveness. We limit our analysis to an admission of our biases; biases which reinforce our original contention: that the type of adult a society desires, determines–to a large extent–how that child is treated in general.

It has been argued that since our society is pluralistic, it is difficult to determine what would constitute a "desirable adult." Our position is that the desirable adult–particularly one of the middle class designation–would be an individual who desires to move into the ranking of the upper class. The middle class individual therefore "guesses" at what attributes would be desirable; which no doubt includes extreme positions of public altruism and private attitudes of intense competitiveness. He or she would then proceed to inculcate these characteristics, disregarding the desires, developmental status, and temperament of a child that is attached to it. As such, the child would learn these attitudes and "role play" them out, automatically adopting them as their own "model of behavior." The result: "Like father, like son; like mother, like daughter." In our view, this disregard–and its attendant results on the child–constitutes flagrant child abuse.

A case in point will illustrate. An upper middle class American family raised their son to be a lawyer. As the son developed professionally, he joined various clubs and organizations that would enhance his position in society. He was, however, unable to marry a woman from a wealthy family, and so married an educated, middle class woman. They had a child, but both continued their careers. As the man steadily moved forward, his behavior–while not illegal–was often seen by his colleges as bordering on the unethical. Yet this man attended church, did not have extramarital affairs, nor did he drink alcoholic beverages of any kind. His only visible problems were his being 50-60 pounds overweight, and his penchant for stretching legal ethics in order to increase his chances of becoming wealthy and powerful. We consider such an adult individual as one who was emotionally abused by his parents and society during his childhood years.

In the case of this individual, the abuse he experienced during his formative years centered around the issue of love and acceptance. Consequently, he only felt loved and wanted when he succeeded. And success in this instance meant not for self or according to his own dictates, but for the "model" of success imposed upon him by his parents, and by the society in which he was raised. For this man–as for so many countless others–American "altruism" thus becomes defined as that life pattern which seeks to blindly obey authority– those reigning models, their characteristics and their attendant considerations–at the expense of the overall health and happiness of the individual.

In our opinion, such a model–and its projection upon a child by its parents and the society in which it is raised–constitutes abuse of the worst type. In reality, a child needs to feel unconditional love in order to grow and develop into the type of human being we, in this American society of ours, *claim–*

that is, *posture*–we want the individual to become. As a child matures, he or she needs to feel that their dignity and rights are respected. If he or she does not feel this to be the case, they have no "model" to follow; to emulate; to act according to; to use in relating equitably to others, thereby instilling these healthful, life-enhancing behaviors in those "others." Even worse, they have little or no empathy for others. Other people are simply seen as resources to be used, abused and disregarded, much in the same way the child was.

If, on the other hand, you want a child who is unethical, conforming in most matters, has a poor self image and is overweight, we have provided you with a good formula for achieving success in this dark endeavor.

While it is difficult for us to get worked up emotionally or to feel sorry for the adult individual portrayed in this example, the picture which we painted here is no different as to the lack of respect and regard shown to the child of a parent who is verbally or physically abusive.

Our contention here is thus simple: this general attitude; that lack of regard and respect for a child, is the single Cause for all exploitative behavior. Our successful lawyer is anxious, depressed, hostile, and overweight. Effects follow Cause, as surely as night follows day.

Chapter 6
The Family as the Cause of Abuse

The primary cause of abuse and neglect is the family and the socialization process that it supports and that supports it.

By "family," we mean the authoritarian male-dominated family model, i.e., that immediate, fundamental, social unit consisting of one dominant male, one manipulative female, and their offspring.

The American family system is–in point of fact–a no- option system. *The term "family" in America is co-extensive with the male dominant-monogamous family model as defined above. This paradigm is continually addressed in the media, with special emphasis being placed upon it during holiday seasons. The President and his family encouraging, promulgating, and reinforcing "approved" American social and religious standards in televised presentations to the American public, is one such example of this media holiday ploy.*

Multiple female or male, homosexual, mixed individuals and single individuals are excluded both socially and morally from such consideration, in addition to their frequently being denied the legal status of "family." As a consequence and an example, and until recently the Internal Revenue Service does not recognize such social structural associations as being legal tax entities.

Thus, they either have no legal status, and few protections, and are regarded as morally inferior to the male-dominated, passive-manipulative female social structural association designated legally as a "family" unit.

Such attitudes and legal measures clearly show American to be the last great stronghold of extolled "individualism:" an individualism that is still based upon an old slavery creed model. We say this, because these espoused creeds not only claim freedom, respect, regard, and love to be the salient virtues of this "democracy," but that these qualities are dispensed equally without regard to "race, color, creed, or–now, and in the most vacuous of ways–sexual orientation." Any perceptive, world-experienced individual reading this book, knows these claims of "equality" and human "consideration for all," to be nothing but utter fabrications and thoughtfully engineered lies, generated and perpetuated by the reigning governmental order and social system under which we currently live.

This difference between idealistic proclamation versus empirical social attitude and action, has turned us into a schizophrenic society; one whose primary defense mechanism is *denial*. That is, while our society shows great concern when it comes to intentionally inflicted violence, this concern is not generalized to the family or legal system as a rule (although it must be remembered that at one time being against capital punishment was in vogue.)

The idea of "family" as it exists in America today, is still most accurately reflected in the old cliché, "A man's home is his castle." And it is true. For in his "castle," a man is indeed lord and master; not only is he the lord over his physical property, but he is the master over those who dwell under its roof, and within its walls.

Psychological Desertion

"Psychological Availability" refers to that condition in which the parent is able to "be there" for the child, in terms of providing it with essential information and strong emotional support. While parents are frequently physically available for their children, sadly the norm–when it comes to "Psychological Availability"–is that they are primarily absent in an emotional sense.

The Illusion of Success in The Abused Child

There has been much said about "Abuse-Resistant" children, a purely American concept and term. The measure for such resistance has often been the observation that some severely abused children seem to have a better-than-average life. While this may be true in terms of the direct measure of their social status in terms of ranking in educational and monetary matters, there has been very little work done that demonstrates the soundness of the emotional structure and identity of these individuals. On the contrary. Our experience has indicated quite the opposite: such children have–at best– a "cold," "offish," or inappropriate set of emotional reactions to different external stimulants (social interactions), in addition to displaying an ill or vaguely defined sense of self (individual identity.)

I have coached over 200 people over a 12 year period. Over half of these individuals have a college education and earned salaries that greatly exceeded the national average. All of these people were psychologically or physically abused, or both. The only difference between these wealthier people and their less educated and wealthy counterparts, were the "toys" and experiences that they were able to purchase or procure in order to better cope with their pain. In addition, these more well-to-do people were somewhat more reluctant even to admit that they were angry. Thus, the less wealthy people displayed an open anger toward the "system" as a whole, while the middle and upper class people simply spent more money on their devices of self-manipulation, in addition to their making up better lies as to why they were not "angry."

Many of these abused individuals were not even aware that they were abused. They thought the behavior their parents and other adults inflicted upon them while they were growing up was indeed "normal"–even "necessary" or "earned" by them, in some way. Like most abused children, they blamed themselves for the abusive treatment they received during their formative years.

Further, it was interesting to find that some of these people believed that it was wrong for them to even say "bad" things about their parents.

Adult Standards and Ideas Cannot be Applied to Children

Much of our discontent with children is based on the tacit assumption that they are simply little adults who deliberately disobey us. Nothing can be further from the truth. They are not "little adults." They are young human beings who are going through a very complicated and natural development cycle, and a very well calculated social development process. Children do not even develop a sense of what adults term "morality" until about the age of eight or nine years of age. And even then, their intellectual comprehension of this code of conduct is not the "same" as that of a sixteen year old teenager, and certainly, nowhere near the developmental state of a thirty-year old adult.

Anthropomorphic type statements and ideas are consistently applied to children. They are frequently called selfish, lazy and irresponsible. Frequently we use these anthropomorphic statements to justify behavior which we would not ordinarily find acceptable or tolerate. Terms such as these are adult generated and can only be applied to adults.

Unconditional Love The Vaccine Against Future Dysfunctions

Other than birth defects and extreme genetic abnormalities, dysfunctional behavior is the first and foremost result of an infant not receiving unconditional love. In order for a healthy adult to emerge from childhood, unconditional acceptance and love are essential elements. If these are lacking, the child develops a chronic fight or flight response which we often refer to as "fear" or "hatred." And deeply embedded within this mind-set of fear and hatred, are the psychological traumas of shame and guilt.

When love is contingent upon behaviors, the child, with its limited means of understanding, feels it is at a loss for obtaining it. Thus he or she accepts, without questioning the vision of the adult; no matter how damning that vision and words might be.

Thus, love takes on the role of a commodity: an "article for sale," no different from any other "thing," an attitude which, in our adult, Western World, is the driving force behind all human actions and interactions.

Unconditional love for the infant is next to impossible in a society which is so preoccupied with performance.

When the psyche of a child has been abused, the adult child of the dysfunctional family feels shame. And as a consequence, a devaluation of oneself is the result. The result is adult children become obsessed with success, looks, and compulsive behaviors; self-protective measures used to fill the "love void" within. This vacuous state creates a discontinuity within their psychological structure.

Parents, regardless of their intentions, desires, dreams, educations or hopes, cannot provide unconditional love if they themselves did not receive it when they were infants and small children. In reality, ***Unconditional love is the vaccine against all future dysfunction.***

The result of not receiving unconditional love as an infant and a small child, eventually and inevitably leads to severe anxiety and depression which, causes a desperate search for relief and fulfillment. However, relief alone is not sufficient to guarantee fulfillment as an adult, since adults raised in this system are often incapable of providing unconditional love to another adult (let alone to a child.) Thus, non-human substitutes which promise relief and tease of possible fulfillment are sought. As is all too often the case, these replacements, ranging from the acquisition of possessions to drug abuse and numerous destructive relationships, are almost always ineffective substitutes.

Social status, power, wealth, education–all become substitutes for this unconditional love. But since the individual can no longer feel the void within *directly*, the chase to obtain these replacements eventually becomes overtaken by the fear of failure. A fear that not only will these replacements elude them, but, that if they are "eventually" or "somehow" attained, they will prove be "anti-climactic." That is, the individual senses that their attainment will not fill their growing, desperate and often growing void within.

None of this is to say that social status, power, and wealth cannot be pursued as things in themselves. But in this context it must be remembered that sand is no substitute for water.

Frustration thus becomes the final state of the suffering individual, and nothing in this world appears capable of filling that growing, intensely black void within. It is also true, as our newspapers testify to nearly every day, that those individuals who claim the need for unconditional love can be only filled by our Western religions, have completely deluded themselves. We say this because as those newspapers have clearly shown, Western religion is now known to be more of a cause for child abuse than it is a cure. And this, in the most physical forms of child molestation, as well as of the emotional destruction and mental abuse that flows from such treatment by those are sworn to "Suffer not these little ones to come unto Me..." (Matthew 19:14) Individuals who believe that the need for unconditional love and acceptance can be filled by obsession with possessions are also facing further disappointment.

One case comes to mind which illustrates this point. I was invited by a family into their home to train their son. When I arrived, I was duly impressed with both the home's location and size. The house was enormous it was a mansion.

The child had every conceivable toy and device imaginable, as well as the constant attention of a personal maid. The father and mother however, were both heavily addicted to amphetamines and alcohol, as well as to the most dialectical forms of materialism. Both parents came from middle class families who strongly instilled the "success ethic" into each of them. Neither one had ever felt loved as a child, yet this was initially and heavily denied. When these parents were asked how they knew they were loved when they were children, both talked about the many things their parents did for them, and the opportunities their parents gave them. It was obvious that despite their opulent lifestyle, both of these parents lived their mental and emotional lives in the blackest of personally-made hells; pits of despair and emptiness, into which they had "lovingly" tossed their own offspring. An offspring who was being prepared to faithfully and "righteously" carry out the "family tradition."

The "A-Team"

Unlike the famous A-Team, (in the 1980s) which righted wrongs and served justice, the "A-Team" in this context stands for the "Abuse Team." Why this designation? Because abusive behavior becomes a "team activity" that includes both enablers and co-dependents.

The child's bonding to the parent creates a co-dependent situation which causes the child to become part of the abuse syndrome.

In other words, because the child needs the adult parents for its survival, the child assumes that whatever a parent does is appropriate and justified. Thus, in most cases, children regard abusive behavior as "normal and natural." Is it any wonder then, that when they become adults, they do not regard their parents as having been abusive toward them when they were children?

This natural assumption makes it difficult to treat many abused children. Denying abuse not only serves the purpose of reducing conscious pain in the abused, but also helps to maintain the illusory bond of love which the child requires in order to hold its sense of identity together. In fact, most abused children go so far as to question the actual reality and cause of their abuse. That is, when abused, they wonder what they "did wrong" to "earn" the "punishment" they received.

"In case studies I conducted of well over two hundred and fifty abused adults, only five to six percent did not deny that they were abused. Of this group, only 1 person labeled their parents' abusive and destructive behavior as immoral and sick."

The other approximately ninety-four percent believed that no matter what their parents did to them, the "punishment" they received was not only justified, but was actually deserved. This ranged from merciless beatings, sexual contact, slapping, and name calling, to chronic personality attacks. This last category comprised the majority of my patient population. No matter how successful these patients were, they felt a fundamental sense of worthless and shame. About one half of them were sports figures, doctors, nurses, police officers, psychotherapists, lawyers, and successful business people. They drove new cars, had beautiful homes, money and clothes. And yet, they never felt satisfied or fulfilled by any of their successes, or with any of their possessions. Rather, they were constantly plagued with the most intense fears and doubts. Most of them were completely immoral, abused drugs, alcohol, and food, had numerous affairs, gambled, lied and cheated.

I can remember one well known star who constantly harmed himself by cutting his own body. When asked about his parents and his childhood, all he could say was that his parents provided him with everything, and that he could not understand why he was still so unhappy. He was referred to a physician who found nothing physically wrong with him. He was then referred to a psychoanalyst. After a number of years of treatment, he was still cutting himself, although less frequently. Even so, he still had no insight into his difficulties. He simply continued to blame himself, and in the process, managed to misuse every psychological concept he learned from his analyst to find further fault with himself.

It is essential to emphasize that because the child is a member of the Abusive Team, he or she is neither responsible nor guilty for the abuse visited upon him or her, regardless of how difficult a child he or she might be. Only adults can be held responsible for abusive behavior.

The Abuse Team (AT) also consists of other individuals: those family members, neighbors (and society itself for that matter) who do not intervene in order to save the child from abusive behavior, and the inevitable, life-long suffering it leads to.

Nevertheless, the child is usually the greatest defender of its abusers. Frequently, this is a result of denial, as well as a form of amnesia. It is as if the child has been hypnotized by its parents, society and the media, and ordered to ignore or forget all of the episodes and incidents of abuse that were visited upon it. The result of this "forgetting" does not lead to forgiveness or resolution. For in order to forgive; to "let go" and relieve the pain, the individual must first of all, *remember*.

Chapter 7
Some Case Examples of the Inter-generational Transmission of Abusive Behavior

Psychological Pain: Method and Symptom
Symptoms and Origins of Internalized Self-Other Abuse Thought Patterns

Below is a list of thinking and communicating styles that are indicative of those that abuse, and of those that have been abused. Individuals who exhibit two or more of these tendencies are prime candidates for having been abused; at least psychologically, and then passing this abuse on to their children.

1. Always or Never thinking
2. All or Nothing scenarios
3. Over generalizations, non professional diagnosing.
4. Accepting emotional appeals as valid. (If John feels this, then it must be valid)
5. Accepting titles or position as positive proof of assertion
6. Exaggeration or Ignoring
7. Personalization
8. Labeling
9. Should/have to/must ("Shoulda, Coulda, Woulda")
10. Emotional reasoning (because I "feel" this, the premises are true) Used extensively by religious cults to convert followers
11. Mind Reading
12. Prophesying

Those using these forms of internal and external communications techniques, are abusing themselves and others.

These methods of communication, thinking, and reacting, are extrapolations from the authoritarian model discussed previously. And as we know, in Western culture, the authoritarian patriarchal model. Equally, it must be remembered, that the *APM* assumes that man is fundamentally evil by nature. Taken together, the twelve techniques listed above, when coupled to the *APM*–as they most certainly are in daily life–assure an abuse-stream that is perpetuating, generation after generation.

The authoritarian model posits such an ideal of perfection, as to make it impossible for anyone to legitimately feel good about themselves. As the authoritarian model of perfection is–by definition–impossible to reach, we are forced to split ourselves into two distinct, separate psychic selves: that is, literally generate a "private" and "public" self. It is not difficult to understand that such a division not only shatters the possibility of feeling fundamentally worthwhile, but makes intrinsic self-worth contingent upon both performance and image. Individuals compare themselves and others to the "ideal;" and since no one can live up to that "ideal," everyone–including the self–is not only suspect of guilt, but deserving of punishment.

The origin of these authoritarian models are based, of course, in master/slave creeds which, in the West, have their origins in the Judeo-Christian belief systems rooted in the Old and New Testament, as well as in the Eastern Hindu philosophy.

Individuals who use abusive thinking techniques on others, also use the same principles on themselves. It is ironic but true: a person who inflicts psychological pain on others, is also inflicting that same pain on their own self.

The Importance of Owning Your Own Guilt

*The question of real life boundaries:
Guilt and shame that is abuse-based destroys the person's sense of freedom and responsibility...
making it difficult to feel earned guilt and shame...
and making it impossible to make amends*

One of the greatest dangerous of ALL abusive behavior is the submergence of healthy guilt: an internal mechanism designed to release emotional energy and re-balance the ego. Instead, such authentic and healthy guilt is replaced by a sense of "global" guilt and shame. That is, the individual constantly feels a deep sense of guilt and shame, regardless of the issue or matter at hand.

This sense of global guilt and shame rapidly transforms itself into an "escape state." That is, a tendency for one to attempt to escape from genuine responsibility and true freedom. It does not take long for such an "escape" attempt to quickly degenerate into severe bouts of depressions and anxieties. This latter process finally results in defensive and rigid maneuvers devised by the self to protect it–at all costs–from both genuine freedom and true responsibility. In turn, these maneuvers lead to deep and secret feelings of helplessness, self medication, and defensive self-worth manipulations.

It is our opinion, that global guilt and shame are inappropriate, simply because they assign responsibility erroneously. The individual feels guilty and shameful for events and circumstances that are not his or her responsibility in the first place. But the assumption of such responsibility creates within the individual the feeling that they cannot get out from under, except through denial, further psychological self-brutalization, or by their indulging in a generally irresponsible attitude. Global guilt and shame are actually formed during childhood, when the critical and differentiating mental faculties have not yet developed. Thus, events and reactions are accepted or rejected as wholes, leading to overwhelming emotions and character distortions.

Frequently, in attempting to escape from these terrifying feelings, the individual will deny or accept responsibility and blame for almost everything. The famous statement "It's not my problem," or "It's my fault," are nothing more than primitive, rigid defenses against the helplessness created by any type of guilt and shame: whether it is earned or not.

In other words, any form of guilt or shame–whether deserved or not–stimulates the sense of global guilt or shame still further. When this occurs, the person is overwhelmed, and cannot use their critical faculties to differentiate between the "parts" that he or she does own as a consequence of their actions–or due to a lack of action–and those parts that either belong to others, or can rightly be attributed to circumstance. Thus, the avoidance of earned guilt and shame eventually leads to excessive defensive posturing. Even though a person may appear to have shed their earned guilt, in reality, they continue to suffer in silence.

This results in the loss of self-esteem and self-worth. The process is simple: if a person cannot be responsible and thus potentially guilty for his actions, he feels that his actions do not stand for much. When this occurs the person feels a loss of self-esteem and self-worth, as well as a loss of freedom. He is forever in a cycle of burden; demanding that everyone make adjustments for his inability to cope, or by making adjustments for others' inability to cope. It is therefore completely impossible to cope in a productive or healthy way, when global guilt or shame are involved. There is simply no way to pay back the debt.

It is important to note, that both global guilt and shame can be traced back to belief systems which easily interact with a child's normal need to understand and control his world. Rigid world views, generalizations, blaming, labeling, and inappropriate demands however, plant within the child the seeds for becoming a "globalizer."

Becoming fearful of guilt due to the possible consequences of being guilty, appear damning or overwhelming and, in fact, create the type of individual a highly moralistic authoritarian system wants. Such a system does not want people who are free, productive and loving. To the contrary. It *requires* highly anxious individuals who obey. The individual's response to such a system is compulsiveness and global conformity, sneaky rebellion, and symptomology. These can manifest as addictions, psychosomatic disorders, or the violation of the necessary and essential laws needed for interpersonal survival.

Globalizing is operative in all stereotypical and ritualized behaviors. It can easily be observed in new settings, or anywhere where emotional tension is high.

The Non-Specific Effects of An Abusive Culture

**High autonomic reactivity leading to:
addictions as self-medication, phobic reactions, violence, psycho-somatic illness, generalized depression, chronic stress, economic chaos and chronic anxiety**

The *Autonomic Nervous System* (*ANS*) is commonly known as the flight or fight bio-survival system, which is designed to help organisms respond rapidly to life threatening situations. The *ANS* is primarily a non- cognitive system. That is, it does not involve thinking or analytical reasoning. As a consequence, cognitive intervention has a minimal effect.

Each child that is born has an autonomic nervous system (*ANS*) which possesses a particular, wired genetic base-line. This causes some children to respond more heavily to one type of stimulation or bodily condition, than to another.

Except in rare cases, most children's *ANS* baseline falls within a healthy and functional range. The *ANS* baseline can be raised by the circumstances in which a child develops. In other words, since children can not fight successfully with adults, or successfully get along without adult assistance (flight), an environment that continually threatens them will lead to higher than healthy *ANS* baselines. Depending upon the types and the durations of the threat, the *ANS* baseline can be distorted to such an extent, that the child begins to live in a state of chronic tension. After a period of time, this state of chronic tension comes to be regarded as "normal" and "natural" by the child.

The baseline *ANS* can be elevated at any particular period within the child's development process. Frequently, if this occurs over a long period of time and over many developmental stages, numerous external and internal cues will be classically and operationally conditioned to this higher level of arousal. A therapist–whether a Freudian or a Behaviorist–can spend an entire lifetime providing insight and behavioral change with little fundamental modification in the "Baseline *ANS*" or, "*BANS*."

Not only do particular parental reactions effect *BANS*, but–in fact–every culture actually desires a particular *BANS*. For example: a culture such as ours values a higher baseline than does, say, an aboriginal culture.

Americans as a group have a higher baseline then might be desirable, when measured by our levels of psychosomatic illness, violence, suicide, child abuse and a myriad of addictions and compulsions.

Children raised in such environments–regardless of their apparent outward success–are, as we have pointed out earlier, fundamentally dysfunctional. Their *BANS* threshold is very high, predisposing them to various symptoms, as well as inclining them toward various forms of destructive self-medication. Therefore they possess self-destructive characteristics, and often become the cause of much unnecessary pain to their loved ones; in addition to themselves.

It seems obvious that most forms of self-destructive behaviors serve as a primary attempt to reduce the painful effects of a high *BANS* threshold, while in a secondary way, serves to punish or reward the environment or self.

High Autonomic Reactivity (HAR). This term refers to the increased probability of occurrence of an undifferentiated, non-cognitive emotional-thought reaction to a given set of internal and/or external factors. Neither *HAR* nor its reactions have a present tense survival value, although psycho-physiologically the organism reacts "as if" they do.

HAR manifests as a tendency of over-readiness to respond. The process is circular and self-perpetuating. Frequently, people suffering from *HAR*, have been labeled as ultra-sensitive, highly anxious, emotionally flat, depressed, socially incompetent, dull, hostile, unmotivated, fearful, shy, dishonest or manipulative. They appear to be self-absorbed in their own feelings, their belief systems, childhood training, and their interpersonal reactions. Thus the metaphor of "Being *HAR* bound" is appropriate in describing them.

The introduction of logic, reason, and insight, have little lasting effect on these types of people. The level of tension they have become accustomed to experiencing is seen by them as being "normal" and "natural," as is their self- medicating behavior—whether it be toward excessive social contacts, drugs, food, alcohol, or sex or other compulsive behaviors.

Individuals who suffer from *HAR* can correctly be viewed as "self-medicators" and, in fact, make up the majority of the population now known as "addicts."

Frequently being painful, organisms develop defenses to *HAR* in order to reduce the pain. These defenses are most typically developed automatically and without critical evaluation or cognitive intervention. Thus, they continue to operate unobstructed, in addition to being automatically reinforced. The one so afflicted begins to consider *HAR* reactions as natural and necessary, rather than as learned. Such defensive structures fall into two very broad categories known as "Funneled-Confined" and "Barreled-Reactive."

Broadly speaking, the Funneled-Confined type defense tends to restrict input, while the Barrelled-Reactive has difficulty in restricting output.

The automatic and habitual quality of *HAR*, and its correlated defense structures, creates the belief that both the *HAR*-level and its defense structures are the "Self." This unfortunate fact makes it particularly difficult in helping the person, in addition to it giving many clinicians the idea that the person is "resistant to change."

Extreme levels of *HAR* create an internal environment wherein minor external changes take on significant consequences through autonomic feeding. Minor–and in fact non threatening–situations can be built up to catastrophe level, simply because of the generally high level of *HAR*. People who suffer from this phenomenon are indeed very difficult to help, particularly if the therapist pays too close attention to the details of the environmental stimulus, and to the patients explanations of them. In other words, the treating of specific symptoms can be next to useless, until the general level of *HAR* is significantly reduced.

The majority of these *HAR*s have been learned through social interactions. And indeed, the majority of these *HAR*s are expressed through social interactions. Thus, while *HAR* is an interpersonal event, its reactions have been internalized.

Another curious aspect of *HAR*, is that it can inhibit or facilitate learning, while learning can reduce or increase *HAR*. The implication of this is that learning new behavior can generalize to some degree and reduce *HAR*, and that the learning of new behaviors can be inhibited to some degree by *HAR*.

While the above is true, it must be stated that the general state of the person cannot be significantly altered by the learning of new behaviors. This makes normal behavioral re-conditioning of habits and self defeating attitudes difficult at best, since the level of the flight or fight response is continuously high.

Conditionability is also a function of autonomic reactivity. It is different for various types of individuals. That is, some individuals are easier to condition than others. This doesn't imply that re-conditioning cannot alter *HAR*, but it does mean that careful consideration must be given to the various types and patterns of conditioning–as well as to the type of individual involved–in working out a particular treatment program.

It is believed that *HAR* is normally distributed. However, the -1 to -2 standard deviation would be considered the theoretical ideal. In other words, average or normal *HAR* would be considered unhealthy. We assume this, based upon such things as psychosomatic stress related diseases, and the frequency and degree of interpersonal and family dysfunction. Put plainly, the typical American family is regarded as unhealthy, even though it is in the statistical mean.

Diagnosis and treatment is a function of contextual defense structures, type, and present level of organization. Regardless, the goal of therapy is to reduce *HAR* to acceptable levels, without interfering with the creative responses of the person.

Some Case Histories with *HAR*

Ms. Reagan, who is normally bossy, pushy and demanding, experiences some set-backs in her plans. Her behavior changes to passive-dependency, which lasts for about three months. Upon the cessation of the stress, she becomes her old, bossy, pushy and demanding self once again.

The therapist treating her at the time assumed that her compliant and insightful behavior was due to treatment. He too was surprised when her original behavior re- appeared.

Ms. Reagan's normal behavior is a defensive reaction to a high *HAR*. Changes in her personal life threatened her to such a degree, that her *HAR* level became depressed to compensate for perceived threats to her life style. Her new behavior was seen as more socially acceptable to both herself and her therapist. During this phase, she had insights into her behavior which neatly fit the therapist's paradigm, which was probably correct. However, as soon as the outside threat subsided, her original behavior reappeared–*HAR* rose quickly, and to cope with the shift, she reverted to her normal behavioral manner.

Highly aggressive, hostile and anxious individuals normally suffer from a very high *HAR*.

Mr. Bruce arrived in a high state of anxiety. When questioned, he stated that his wife was leaving him. Within two weeks they were back together again. He was very grateful, assuming that therapy he had undergone brought her back to him. While his over-all tension appeared reduced, he was still very compliant and obsequious. While the focus of his anxiety was no longer desertion by his wife, his level of social fearfulness was still extremely high.

As the situation would have it, they split up again. This time he was referred to a behavioral therapist for systematic desensitization, as well as social retraining. When seen a year later he was no longer panicky. However, his levels of anxiety where still high; his social mannerisms being abrupt and tense.

***

A patient was referred to treatment with a diagnosis of paranoid schizophrenia. The patient was rigid and distant, but yet, highly functional. After the patient became acquainted with the therapist, his behavior became more relaxed. He seemed to be making marked improvement. One day he arrived in the office intoxicated. He accused the therapist of trying to destroy his relationship with a woman the therapist once saw him with in the waiting room. The patient accused the therapist of being jealous and abruptly left the office. During the course of treatment, the patient had insights into his ideations, and had made considerable changes in his life. Still, episodes of minimal stress continued to severely overwhelm his cognitive control.

It was later found out that prior to his intoxication, he experienced a minor reversal in the stock market. The stress of the situation was initially "controlled" by the consumption of alcohol, but was soon followed by belligerent and hostile behavior, in addition to paranoid ideation.

***

A housewife sought treatment for a sexual dysfunction. Her complaint was that she became angry with her husband when he washed his mouth out after their oral sex. She perceived and experienced his action as a rejection of her. She repeated over and over again that she would never have sex with him again. She also added that he never could simply hold her without having to engage in sexual activity.

She was diagnosed as having a child-like hysteroid personality disorder. She was a perfectionist, and very judgmental. In short, she was hyper-concerned with what she imagined others thought of her. No amount of empathy, insight, or rational explanation helped her. It was possible to adjust her to her condition by using "shame" as a negative reinforcement, since this patient was already "shamed to death."

Attempts to get her to relax were met with resistance and suspicion. When she was questioned about her childhood, she simply repeated that her childhood was uneventful, and that her parents were wonderful.

After a few sessions, she sought medical treatment. Her physician provided her with tranquilizers. A few years later she was still using them. Her marriage had ended in divorce, and she had gotten involved with a man who was more sensitive. Later, he was found out to be a gigolo, who was simply interested in her money.

These and thousands of other case histories reveal certain patterns of *HAR* which feed and are fed by interpersonal interaction.

***

Most therapies focus on insight, re-training, and catharsis. Although there is some success with treatment, the fundamental level of *HAR* is only slightly reduced. It should also be noted, that almost any stress will re-introduce old symptoms or generate new ones, as the individual attempts to cope with a given stressor.

Other than birth defects and extreme abnormalities, *HAR* is a result of the infant not receiving unconditional love. In order for a healthy adult to emerge from the formative years of early childhood, unconditional acceptance and love are essential. If this is lacking, the organism develops a chronic flight or fight response, which we normally call "fear" or "hatred."

Love which is held to be contingent upon behavior, is not love at all. The child–with its limited means of understanding adult behavior–feels it is at a loss of obtaining it, and comes to think that there is "something" lacking in its natural self; something that is unlovable, and which must be paid for with such and such behaviors or actions. Thus, love takes on the role of a contingent "commodity" which–in the adult Western World is the standard, as we have previously explained.

"Unconditional love for the infant is next to impossible in a society which is so preoccupied with performance"

The result of not receiving unconditional love as an infant and small child, leads to severe anxiety and depression which–in turn–leads to a desperate search for relief and fulfillment. However, "relief" alone is not sufficient to guarantee "fulfillment" as an adult, since adults raised in this system are often incapable of providing unconditional love to another adult (let alone to a child.) Consequently, non-human substitutes are sought: ranging from, food addictions, possessions, alcohol, drugs, compulsive behaviors such as gambling, addiction to pornography, etc.

"Unconditional love is typically experienced as a feeling of deep joy, coupled to a sensation of great relaxation."

Unconditional love is typically experienced as a feeling of deep joy, coupled to a sensation of great relaxation. While adults have little to compare this description with, it might be compared to a complete orgasm: something that is also rare in a contingency and performance oriented culture such as ours.

In the latter instance, it should be noted that individuals who claim to have experienced deep and complete orgasm are more often than not fooling themselves. It is easy to test such claims: simply observe the behaviors such claimants exhibit in their day to day activities.

The realization that chronic tension is frequently unobservable by the victim–since he or she has little to compare their "normal" state with–is not a new idea. In the East, numerous techniques were developed to help individuals gain control over their *ANS*. However, the majority of these techniques required years of work, and provided little insight or understanding to the user.

Chapter 8
Treatment and Prevention

MEASURING PSYCHOLOGICAL ABUSE

We have developed a simple paper and pencil testing instrument. At present, this instrument is in its experimental phase, and therefore must be administered and interrupted with some caution.

Below are twenty-one questions which focus on the reader's memory of particular experiences as a child and as an adolescent. *There are no right or wrong answers here.*

You may experience some unpleasant or pleasant emotions or memories while responding to these questions. *Please do not let these feelings bias your honest and open reactions.* If you need to speak to someone about how you feel, we urge you to consult a licensed therapist, or see your family physician.

Although it can be hard, it's critical to be completely honest with yourself. Only you will know your responses and will not be revealed to anyone unless you choose to.

Please answer each question by checking either "YES" or "NO". If you check "YES," then proceed to the second question which refers to the frequency of the event under consideration.

1. As a child, do you remember being labeled[1] or called names?
❏ Yes ❏ No
If you checked No, proceed to the next numbered question.
If you checked Yes, answer the following question.
The highlighted event happened: ❏ Frequently ❏ Rarely
As an adolescent, do you remember being labeled or called names?
❏ Yes ❏ No
If you checked No, proceed to the next numbered question.
If you checked Yes, answer the following question.
The highlighted event happened: ❏ Frequently ❏ Rarely

2. As a child, do you remember being yelled at?
❏ Yes ❏ No
If you checked No, proceed to the next numbered question.
If you checked Yes, answer the following question.
The highlighted event happened: ❏ Frequently ❏ Rarely
As an adolescent, do you remember being yelled at?
❏ Yes ❏ No
If you checked No, proceed to the next numbered question.
If you checked Yes, answer the following question.
The highlighted event happened: ❏ Frequently ❏ Rarely

3. As a child, do you remember being threatened with the withdrawal of love or acceptance?
❏ Yes ❏ No
If you checked No, proceed to the next numbered question.
If you checked Yes, answer the following question.
The highlighted event happened: ❏ Frequently ❏ Rarely
As an adolescent, do you remember being threatened with

---

[1] Labels such as smart, stupid, ugly, beautiful, good, bad, idiot, genius, a fool awful, disgusting, dirty; or sexual comments, sexist labels, etc.

the withdrawal of love or acceptance?
❑ Yes ❑ No
If you checked No, proceed to the next numbered question.
If you checked Yes, answer the following question.
The highlighted event happened: ❑ Frequently ❑ Rarely

4. As a child, do you remember being compared to a sibling, relative, or friend, either in a positive or negative fashion?
❑ Yes ❑ No
If you checked No, proceed to the next numbered question.
If you checked Yes, answer the following question.
The highlighted event happened: ❑ Frequently ❑ Rarely
As an adolescent, do you remember being compared with a sibling, relative, or a friend, in either a positive or negative fashion?
❑ Yes ❑ No
If you checked No, proceed to the next numbered question.
If you checked Yes, answer the following question.
The highlighted event happened: ❑ Frequently ❑ Rarely

5. As a child, do you remember witnessing verbal[2] or physical violence between your parents/caretakers?
❑ Yes ❑ No
If you checked No, proceed to the next numbered question.
If you checked Yes, answer the following question.
The highlighted event happened: ❑ Frequently ❑ Rarely
As an adolescent, do you recall witnessing verbal or physical violence between your parents/caretakers?
❑ Yes ❑ No
If you checked No, proceed to the next numbered question.
If you checked Yes, answer the following question.
The highlighted event happened: ❑ Frequently ❑ Rarely

---

[2] Verbal violence consists of name calling, yelling, screaming and shouting, etc.

6. As a child, do you remember being threatened with violence, abandonment, or institutionalization?
❑ Yes ❑ No
If you checked No, proceed to the next numbered question.
If you checked Yes, answer the following question.
The highlighted event happened: ❑ Frequently ❑ Rarely
As an adolescent, do you remember being threatened with violence, abandonment, or institutionalization?
❑ Yes ❑ No
If you checked No, proceed to the next numbered question.
If you checked Yes, answer the following question.
The highlighted event happened: ❑ Frequently ❑ Rarely

7. As a child, do you remember being beaten, tortured, hit hard, abandoned, or institutionalized?
❑ Yes ❑ No
If you checked No, proceed to the next numbered question.
If you checked Yes, answer the following question.
The highlighted event happened: ❑ Frequently ❑ Rarely
As an adolescent, do you remember being beaten, tortured, hit hard, abandoned, or institutionalized?
❑ Yes ❑ No
If you checked No, proceed to the next numbered question.
If you checked Yes, answer the following question.
The highlighted event happened: ❑ Frequently ❑ Rarely

8. As a child, do you remember being told what your future would be like if you obeyed or did not obey your caretakers or teachers?
❑ Yes ❑ No
If you checked No, proceed to the next numbered question.
If you checked Yes, answer the following question.
The highlighted event happened: ❑ Frequently ❑ Rarely
As an adolescent, do you remember being told what your

future would be like if you obeyed or did not obey your caretakers or teachers?

❏ Yes ❏ No

If you checked No, proceed to the next numbered question.
If you checked Yes, answer the following question.
The highlighted event happened: ❏ Frequently ❏ Rarely

9. As a child, do you remember having the feeling that how your parents felt about themselves was a function of how you turned out?

❏ Yes ❏ No

If you checked No, proceed to the next numbered question.
If you checked Yes, answer the following question.
The highlighted event happened: ❏ Frequently ❏ Rarely
As an adolescent, do you remember having the feeling that how your parents felt about themselves was a function of how you turned out?

❏ Yes ❏ No

If you checked No, proceed to the next numbered question.
If you checked Yes, answer the following question.
The highlighted event happened: ❏ Frequently ❏ Rarely

10. As a child, do you remember feeling that your presence, feelings, thoughts, or ideas were of little importance?

❏ Yes ❏ No

If you checked No, proceed to the next numbered question.
If you checked Yes, answer the following question.
As an adolescent, do you remember feeling that your presence, feelings, thoughts, or ideas were of little importance?

❏ Yes ❏ No

If you checked No, proceed to the next numbered question.
If you checked Yes, answer the following question.
The highlighted event happened: ❏ Frequently ❏ Rarely

11. As a child, do you remember feeling that your caretakers were emotionally unavailable to you?
❏ Yes ❏ No
If you checked No, proceed to the next numbered question.
If you checked Yes, answer the following question..
The highlighted event happened: ❏ Frequently ❏ Rarely
As an adolescent, do you remember feeling that your caretakers were emotionally unavailable to you?
❏ Yes ❏ No
If you checked No, proceed to the next numbered question.
If you checked Yes, answer the following question.
The highlighted event happened: ❏ Frequently ❏ Rarely

12. As a child, do you remember feeling that you had to take care of your caretakers?
❏ Yes ❏ No
If you checked No, proceed to the next numbered question.
If you checked Yes, answer the following question.
The highlighted event happened: ❏ Frequently ❏ Rarely
As an adolescent, do you remember feeling that you had to take care of your caretakers?
❏ Yes ❏ No
If you checked No, proceed to the next numbered question.
If you checked Yes, answer the following question.
The highlighted event happened: ❏ Frequently ❏ Rarely

13. As a child, do you remember being told that you were guilty, shameful, or responsible for the unhappiness or happiness of another person or other people?
❏ Yes ❏ No
If you checked No, proceed to the next numbered question.
If you checked Yes, answer the following question.
The highlighted event happened: ❏ Frequently ❏ Rarely
As an adolescent, do you remember being told that you were

guilty, shameful, or responsible for the unhappiness or happiness of another person or other people?

❏ Yes ❏ No

If you checked No, proceed to the next numbered question.
If you checked Yes, answer the following question.

The highlighted event happened: ❏ Frequently ❏ Rarely

14. As a child, do you remember feeling unsupported by your caretakers when it came to peer-to-peer or adult- to-child conflicts?

❏ Yes ❏ No

If you checked No, proceed to the next numbered question.
If you checked Yes, answer the following question.

The highlighted event happened: ❏ Frequently ❏ Rarely

As an adolescent, do you remember feeling unsupported by your caretakers when it came to peer- to-peer or adult-to-adolescent conflicts?

❏ Yes ❏ No

If you checked No, proceed to the next numbered question.
If you checked Yes, answer the following question.

The highlighted event happened: ❏ Frequently ❏ Rarely

15. As a child, do you remember being spanked, locked away in small spaces, slapped, having your mouth washed out with soap, etc?

❏ Yes ❏ No

If you checked No, proceed to the next numbered question.
If you checked Yes, answer the following question.

The highlighted event happened: ❏ Frequently ❏ Rarely

As an adolescent, do you remember being spanked, locked away in small spaces, slapped, having your mouth washed out with soap, etc?

❏ Yes ❏ No

If you checked No, proceed to the next numbered question.
If you checked Yes, answer the following question.
The highlighted event happened: ❏ Frequently ❏ Rarely

16. As a child, do you remember being humiliated in front of friends, strangers or relatives?
❏ Yes ❏ No
If you checked No, proceed to the next numbered question.
If you checked Yes, answer the following question.
The highlighted event happened: ❏ Frequently ❏ Rarely
As an adolescent, do you remember being humiliated in front of friends, strangers or relatives?
❏ Yes ❏ No
If you checked No, proceed to the next numbered question.
If you checked Yes, answer the following question.
The highlighted event happened: ❏ Frequently ❏ Rarely

17. As a child, do you remember being told how you will turn out as an adult?
❏ Yes ❏ No
If you checked No, proceed to the next numbered question.
If you checked Yes, answer the following question.
The highlighted event happened: ❏ Frequently ❏ Rarely
As an adolescent, do you remember being told how you will turn out as an adult?
❏ Yes ❏ No
If you checked No, proceed to the next numbered question.
If you checked Yes, answer the following question.
The highlighted event happened: ❏ Frequently ❏ Rarely

18. As a child, do you remember feeling fearful that you might be punished by God?

❑ Yes ❑ No
If you checked No, proceed to the next numbered question.
If you checked Yes, answer the following question.
The highlighted event happened: ❑ Frequently ❑ Rarely
As an adolescent, do you remember feeling fearful that you might be punished by God?
❑ Yes ❑ No
If you checked No, proceed to the next numbered question.
If you checked Yes, answer the following question.
The highlighted event happened: ❑ Frequently ❑ Rarely

19. As a child, do you remember being sexually aroused or sexually attached to one or more of your caretakers?
❑ Yes ❑ No
If you checked No, proceed to the next numbered question.
If you checked Yes, answer the following question.
The highlighted event happened: ❑ Frequently ❑ Rarely
As an adolescent, do you remember being sexually aroused or sexually attached to one or more of your caretakers?
❑ Yes ❑ No
If you checked No, proceed to the next numbered question.
If you checked Yes, answer the following question.
The highlighted event happened: ❑ Frequently ❑ Rarely

20. As a child, do you remember being sexually abused or attacked?
❑ Yes ❑ No
If you checked No, proceed to the next numbered question.
If you checked Yes, answer the following question.
The highlighted event happened: ❑ Frequently ❑ Rarely
As an adolescent, do you remember being sexually abused or attacked?
❑ Yes ❑ No

*If you checked No, proceed to the next numbered question.
If you checked Yes, answer the following question.*
The highlighted event happened: ❏ Frequently ❏ Rarely

21. As a child, do you remember feeling unwanted, unloved or rejected?
❏ Yes ❏ No
*If you checked No, proceed to the next numbered question.
If you checked Yes, answer the following question.*
The highlighted event happened: ❏ Frequently ❏ Rarely
As an adolescent, do you remember feeling unwanted, unloved or rejected?
❏ Yes ❏ No
*If you checked No, proceed to the next numbered question.
If you checked Yes, answer the following question.*
The highlighted event happened: ❏ Frequently ❏ Rarely

Understanding your responses

To determine your score, give "1" point to each "Yes" checked, and multiply it by a number "1" through "5." To determine which number to use, see below:

Frequently 5 4 3 2 1 **Rarely**

For example. If you checked "Yes" for question 10, and you checked number three on the frequency scale, your total score would be "3."

Add up your scores for each question you answered to get final score.

The higher the total score, the greater the probability that you exhibit one or more compulsions or syndromes.

It is important to remember that, since events are correlated or associated, no scientific statement about cause-and-effect relationships can strictly be drawn, even though such a connection may appear plausible. For that was the premise for writing this book: that psychological abuse *is* the causative agent leading to the painful conditions listed below.

Chemicals:

Misuse of drugs and alcohol for self medication purposes (reduction of pain).

Mental obsessions:

These include: sexual and self-mutilation fantasies, violent thoughts, theft, chronic painful memories, or pedophilic desires.

Inter-personal compulsions:

Numerous unhappy marriages and/or relationships, lack of sexual control, excessive socializing, isolation or employment problems, self sacrificial behavior, and interpersonal narcissism.

Psychosomatic symptoms:

Single or multiple psychosomatic diseases, chronic anxiety, chronic depression, insomnia, etc.

Character disorders:

Paranoid ideation, withdrawal, narcissistic strategies, schizophrenic processes, and controlling behavior.

Acting out disorders:

These include violent behavior, ranging from petty theft to murder.

Abusive behavior:

Having the tendency toward acting abusively toward others and one's self.

Again, the reader should be warned that the results of this questionnaire are based on patient reports and charts, and have not been generated from well controlled scientific studies.

Chapter 10
Identifying and Understanding Child Abuse

Any intentional harm, neglect or mistreatment of a child is considered child abuse.

Child abuse is:

Physical abuse. Physical child abuse occurs when a child is purposely physically injured and put at risk of harm by another person.

Sexual abuse. Any sexual activity with a child is child sexual abuse. This can involve sexual contact, such as intentional sexual touching, oral-genital contact or intercourse. This can also involve noncontact sexual abuse of a child, such as exposing a child to sexual activity or pornography. Filming a child in a sexual manner; sexual harassment of a child; or prostitution of a child, including sex trafficking are all sexual abuse.

Emotional abuse. Emotional child abuse means injuring a child's self-esteem or emotional well-being. It includes verbal and emotional assault. Continually belittling or berating a child is abuse. Isolating, ignoring or rejecting a child is abusive and detrimental to their well-being and normal development. Trying to control children by withholding approval or love unless they behave the way you want them is psychological abuse.

Medical abuse. Medical child abuse occurs when someone gives false information about illness in a child that requires medical attention, putting the child at risk of injury and unnecessary medical care.

Neglect. Failure to provide adequate food, clothing, shelter, clean living conditions, affection, supervision, education, or dental or medical care are symptoms of child neglect. Another form of neglect is to live in an environment where adults are taking drugs, drinking alcohol and thus creating an unsafe home for the child. In many cases, child abuse is done by someone the child knows, such as a parent, relative or family friend. The child can be vulnerable to abuse from others if the parent is neglectful.

An abused child may feel guilty, ashamed or confused. The child may be afraid to tell anyone about the abuse, especially if the abuser is a parent, other relative or family friend.

That's why it's vital to watch for red flags, such as:

- Withdrawal from friends or usual activities
- Changes in behavior: such as aggression, anger, hostility or hyperactivity or changes in school performance
- Depression, anxiety or fear, or a sudden loss of self-confidence
- Sleep problems and nightmares
- Frequent absences from school
- Rebellious or defiant behavior
- Self-harm or attempts at suicide

The presence of warning signs doesn't necessarily mean that a child is being abused, but it's wise to take note.

Physical abuse signs and symptoms
- Unexplained injuries, such as bruises, broken bones (fractures) or burns
- Injuries that don't match the given explanation
- Injuries that aren't compatible with the child's developmental ability

Sexual abuse signs and symptoms
- Sexual behavior or knowledge that's inappropriate for the child's age
- Pregnancy or a sexually transmitted infection
- Genital or anal pain, bleeding, or injury
- Statements by the child that he or she was sexually abused
- Inappropriate sexual behavior with other children
- Emotional abuse signs and symptoms
- Delayed or inappropriate emotional development
- Loss of self-confidence or self-esteem
- Social withdrawal or a loss of interest or enthusiasm
- Depression
- Avoidance of certain situations, such as refusing to go to school or ride the bus
- Appears to desperately seek affection
- A decrease in school performance or loss of interest in school
- Loss of previously acquired developmental skills

Symptoms of Neglect
- Poor growth
- Excessive weight with medical complications that are not being adequately addressed
- Poor personal cleanliness
- Lack of clothing or supplies to meet physical needs
- Hoarding or stealing food

- Poor record of school attendance
- Lack of appropriate attention for medical, dental or psychological problems or lack of necessary follow-up care

Parental behavior

Sometimes a parent's attitude or behavior sends red flags about child abuse. Warning signs include a parent who:

- Shows little concern for the child
- Appears unable to recognize physical or emotional distress in the child
- Blames the child for the problems
- Consistently belittles or berates the child, and describes the child with negative terms, such as "worthless" or "evil"
- Expects the child to provide attention and care to the parent and seems jealous of other family members getting attention from the child
- Uses harsh physical discipline
- Demands an inappropriate level of physical or academic performance
- Severely limits the child's contact with others
- Uses the child as a personal servant instead of letting them play
- Avoids the duties of parenting by making the child take total responsibility for younger siblings
- Offers conflicting or unconvincing explanations for a child's injuries or no explanation at all
- Repeatedly brings the child for medical evaluations or medical tests, such as X-rays and lab tests, for concerns not seen during the health care provider's examination

Physical punishment

Child health experts condemn the use of violence in any form, but some people still use physical punishment, such as spanking, slapping, or whipping to discipline their children. While parents and caregivers use physical punishment with the excuse of helping their children or making their behavior better, research shows that spanking is linked with worse, not better, behavior. It's also linked to mental health problems, difficult relationships with parents, lower self-esteem and lower academic performance.

Any physical punishment may leave emotional scars. Parental behaviors that cause pain, physical injury or emotional trauma, could be child abuse.

When to seek help

If you're concerned that your child or another child has been abused, seek help immediately. Depending on the situation, contact the child's health care provider, a local child welfare agency, the police department or a 24-hour hotline for advice. In the United States, you can get information and assistance by calling or texting the Childhelp National Child Abuse Hotline at **1-800-422-4453**.

If the child needs immediate medical attention, call 911 or your local emergency number.

In the United States, keep in mind that health care professionals and many other people, such as teachers and social workers, are legally required to report all suspected cases of child abuse to the appropriate local child welfare agency.

Physical and psychological effects of child abuse

Some children overcome the physical and psychological effects of child abuse, particularly those with strong social support and resiliency skills who can adapt and cope with bad experiences. For many others, child abuse may result in lifelong physical, behavioral, emotional or mental health issues. Here are some examples.

Physical issues
Premature death
Physical disabilities
Learning disabilities
Substance abuse
Health problems, such as heart disease, diabetes, chronic lung disease and cancer
Behavioral issues
Illegal or violent behavior
Abuse of others
Withdrawal
Suicide attempts or self-injury
High-risk sexual behaviors or teen pregnancy
Problems in school or not finishing high school
Limited social and relationship skills
Problems with work or staying employed
Emotional issues
Low self-esteem
Difficulty establishing or maintaining relationships
Challenges with intimacy and trust
An unhealthy view of parenthood
Inability to cope with stress and frustrations
An acceptance that violence is a normal part of relationships
Mental health disorders
Eating disorders
Personality disorders
Behavior disorders
Depression
Anxiety disorders
Post-traumatic stress disorder (PTSD)
Trouble sleeping (insomnia) and nightmares
Attachment disorders

Identification and Prevention

You can avoid abusing a child by becoming educated, being aware and sensitive to the issue. Take steps to protect your child from exploitation and child abuse, as well as prevent child abuse in your neighborhood or community. The goal is to provide safe, stable, nurturing relationships for children.

Keep children safe:

Give your child love and attention. Children need nurturing. Listen to your child and be involved in their life to develop trust and good communication. Encourage your child to tell you if there's a problem. A supportive family environment and social networks can help improve your child's feelings of self-esteem and self-worth.

Don't inflict your anger on your children. If you feel overwhelmed or out of control, take a break. Don't take your anger out on your child. Talk with a therapist or counselor about ways you can learn to cope with stress and better interact with your child.

Be responsible. Don't leave a young child home alone. In public, keep a close eye on your child. Volunteer at school and for activities to get to know the adults who spend time with your child. Think carefully before leaving your child alone with people you don't know very well. When old enough to go out without supervision, encourage your child to stay away from strangers and to hang out with friends rather than be alone. Make it a rule that your child tells you where he or she is at all times. Find out who's supervising your child, for example, at a sleepover.

Know your child's caregivers. Check references for babysitters and other caregivers. Make irregular, but frequent, unannounced visits to observe what's happening. Don't allow substitutes for your usual child care provider if you don't know the substitute.

Emphasize when to say no. Make sure your child understands that he or she doesn't have to do anything that seems scary or uncomfortable. Encourage your child to leave a threatening or frightening situation immediately and seek help from a trusted adult. If something happens, encourage your child to talk to you or another trusted adult about what happened. Assure your child that it's OK to talk and that he or she won't get in trouble.

Teach your child how to stay safe online. Put the computer in a common area of your home, not the child's bedroom. Use the parental controls to restrict the types of websites your child can visit. Check your child's privacy settings on social networking sites. Consider it a red flag if your child is secretive about online activities.

Cover online ground rules, such as not sharing personal information; not responding to inappropriate, hurtful or frightening messages; and not arranging to meet an online contact in person without your permission. Tell your child to let you know if an unknown person makes contact through a social networking site. Report online harassment or inappropriate senders to your service provider and local authorities, if necessary.

Reach out. Meet the families in your neighborhood, including parents and children. Develop a network of supportive family and friends. If a friend or neighbor seems to be struggling, offer to baby sit or help in another way. Consider joining a parent support group so that you have an appropriate place to vent your frustrations.

If you're concerned that you might abuse your child, seek help immediately. In the United States, you can get information and assistance by calling or texting the Childhelp National Child Abuse Hotline at **1-800-422-4453**. There are numerous other resources you can find online for help with child abuse issues.

Or you can start by talking with your family health care provider. Your provider may offer a referral to a parent education class, counseling or a support group for parents to help you learn appropriate ways to deal with your anger. If you're misusing alcohol or drugs, ask your health care provider about treatment options.

If you were abused as a child, get counseling to ensure you don't continue the abuse cycle or teach those destructive behaviors to your child.

Remember, child abuse is preventable, and often a symptom of a problem that may be treatable.